"I enjoy reading Phil M_
Jesus and the Christia_
and wit."

Nicky Gumbel, founder of
Trinity Brompton

"The Bible is an amazing and wonderful book, but where do you start reading such a huge tome? Melvin Bragg says that the Bible is 'the most influential book there has ever been in the history of language.' Allow Phil to take you into its story and show you what it's all about. You won't regret it."

Terry Virgo, founder of the Newfrontiers church network

"Phil Moore has very capably distilled the essence of the Scriptures. If you want to get a grip on the Bible, this is a great place to start."

R.T. Kendall, theologian and author of **Sermon on the Mount**

"Bold, fresh, fast-moving, relevant and often controversial, The Bible in 100 Pages gives you the best of Phil Moore, and the best of the Bible. An excellent resource for anyone wanting to get their heads round the biblical story."

Andrew Wilson, author of **If God, Then What?**

THE BIBLE

IN 100 PAGES

SEEING THE BIG PICTURE IN GOD'S GREAT STORY

PHIL MOORE

MONARCH
BOOKS

Oxford, UK & Grand Rapids, Michigan, USA

Published by Monarch Books
an imprint of
Lion Hudson plc
Wilkinson House, Jordan Hill Road,
Oxford OX2 8DR, England
Email: monarch@lionhudson.com
www.lionhudson.com/monarch

ISBN 978 0 85721 551 2
e-ISBN 978 0 85721 552 9

First edition 2014

Acknowledgments
Scripture quotations taken from the *Holy Bible, New
International Version*, copyright © 1973, 1978, 1984, 2011
International Bible Society. Used by permission of Hodder
& Stoughton, a member of the Hodder Headline Group. All
rights reserved. 'NIV' is a trademark of International Bible
Society. UK trademark number 1448790.

A catalogue record for this book is available from the
British Library

Printed and bound in the UK, September 2014, LH26

CONTENTS

INTRODUCTION: SEEING THE BIG PICTURE

Life is short and life is busy. It's very easy to miss the big picture. Some people spend their whole lives climbing up a ladder, only to discover far too late that the ladder has been leaning against the wrong wall.

Nobody ever intends to neglect the things which really matter. We get caught in the headlights of a busy world, like a rabbit on a busy highway, and we freeze. We allow other people to dictate what should fill up our thinking time. A study conducted by the University of Southern California in 2011 suggests we are bombarded with enough information every day to fill the pages of 174 newspapers. It's no wonder that we shut down our senses and ignore many of the messages which cry out for our attention.

Most people want to discover the message of the Bible. The problem is simply that they are too busy. They view the Bible in the same way that I view Leo Tolstoy's *War and Peace*: I know I ought to read it but, frankly, it just looks far too long. That's why I have written this book to help you, whether you are a believer or a non-believer who is simply curious about the book which has shaped so much of what is good in Western culture. As Richard Dawkins, who is certainly no lover of religion, told the King James Bible Trust in February 2010: *"We are a Christian culture. We come from a Christian culture, and not to know the King James Bible is to be, in some small way, barbarian."*

The Bible is unique among the writings of the world. It was written across 2,000 years by at least 44 different authors in 3 languages in 9 countries in 3 continents.[1] It speaks with the varied voices of kings and nomads and shepherds and generals and queens and mothers and poets and thinkers and fishermen – but it also speaks with one consistent voice from start to finish. The reason we get confused when we read the Bible is that we miss the big picture of this start-to-finish story. We are like the person who comes into a room halfway through a movie and then starts complaining that the plot is hard to follow. That's why I have summarized the overarching message of the Bible's 66 books, 1,189 chapters and 31,102 verses into just 100 pages for you. I want to help you to see the big picture in the world's greatest story so that you can discover your own place in the story too.

So get ready for a fast-paced journey through the book which has sold more copies, created more leaders, inspired more poetry, shaped more laws and changed more lives than any other book in history. Get ready to be challenged and encouraged and enlightened and provoked by the big picture of its message. The German monk and Bible scholar Martin Luther claimed that *"The Bible is alive, it speaks to me; it has feet, it runs after me; it has hands, it lays hold of me."* My prayer is that, as you read this book, the living message of the Bible will captivate your own heart too.

Phil Moore
London, April 2014

---

1   The Old Testament was written in Hebrew, with the exception of a few chapters in Daniel and Ezra and one verse in Jeremiah, which are all in Aramaic. The New Testament was written entirely in Greek.

PART 1
CREATURES

GENESIS 1–11
CREATION TO 2200 BC

The Bible begins with God. It's very simple. It doesn't try to convince us that God exists. It doesn't feel it has to. It simply informs us that *"In the beginning God…"*

These first four words of the Bible launch into a chapter which celebrates the incomparable greatness of the Creator God. Genesis 1 tells us ten times that *"God said,"* and it informs us that as a result *"it was so."* God doesn't sweat or struggle to create the world. Even though cosmologists tell us that there are at least 170 billion galaxies in the universe, Genesis 1:16 only uses two Hebrew words when it tells us that *"He also made the stars."* The Bible begins with a mighty declaration that God is God and we are not. God is the Creator and we are his creatures. That's the big picture.

Humans only step onto the stage of world history as God is putting the finishing touches to his work of creation. He creates Adam and Eve in his own image, but what really strikes us is how very different they are from their Creator. The Lord never grows tired or weary (Isaiah 40:28), but humans do. We have to stop at least three times a day to eat food and recharge our strength. God never needs to sleep (Psalm 121:4), but we do. Even if we manage to pull the occasional all-nighter, we always end up paying for it later. The rhythm of our lives cries out that God is God and we are not. We need to spend half of our short lives sleeping, eating and relaxing. That's not just weird. It is deliberate.

Genesis 1 underlines this difference by reminding us six times that the Hebrew day began and ended with nightfall. It is a statement that, by the time we get to work in the morning, God has already punched a twelve-hour shift without us! In case we miss this, God decrees that the seventh day of creation will be a day of rest, a Sabbath. He does not do so because he is tired from six days of exertion. Jesus tells us in Mark 2:27 that *"The Sabbath was made for humans"*. God wanted Adam and Eve to begin their lives resting in a garden they had not planted, picking fruit they had not grown and enjoying food they had not cultivated. The weekly Sabbath would remind them to *"Be still, and know that I am God"* (Psalm 46:10). God is the Creator and we are his creatures. That's the message of Part 1 of the Bible.

This was the issue which the Devil targeted when he disguised himself as a snake and came to tempt Adam and Eve in Genesis 3. They should have known better than to trust a talking snake, but the Devil's message was one which people always like to hear. He encouraged them to play at being God.

The Devil encouraged Adam and Eve to doubt God's Word, asking them, *"Did God really say, 'You must not eat from any tree in the garden'?"* He encouraged them to distrust God's character, maligning his motives by suggesting that *"God knows that when you eat from it your eyes will be opened, and you will be like God."* Finally he denied God's Word outright: *"You will not die."* When Adam and Eve ate the forbidden fruit, they fell under the curse of sin. The bitter aftertaste of the Devil's food was death and sickness and stress and pain and toil – the very opposite of relaxing in the perfect world which God had created.

This sets the scene for the rest of Genesis 1–11. The human population grows and people choose whether to rest in the fact that they are God's dependent creatures or to fight against him in order to become little gods themselves. We can tell that we are still caught up in the struggle from the way that we react when we read the words "dependent creatures". We get offended by the suggestion that we are dependent upon anyone, but that's precisely the point. We could not survive an hour without the breath or heartbeat which God gives us. Even when we play at being little gods, we are only able to do so because the Creator God sustains us in his patient love.

Adam and Eve try to cover over their sin by making clothes from fig leaves, but they can no more save themselves than create themselves. The fully clothed Adam confesses to God that *"I was afraid because I was naked."* They only find forgiveness when the Creator God reveals that he is the Saviour God too. He kills an innocent animal – the first death in the Garden of Eden – and covers their nakedness with clothing made from the hide of the world's first blood sacrifice.

Adam and Eve teach their children that this is how sin must always be forgiven. When their eldest son Cain tries to impress God with the work of his own hands, God points to his younger brother Abel's sacrifice of an innocent lamb and asks him: *"Why is your face downcast? If you do what is right, will you not be accepted?"*[1] Cain is faced with a choice: Will he accept that God is God and he is not? He prefers to be a self-assertive murderer than a dependent creature. He kills his brother and founds a dynasty of rebels who try to act like little human gods.

Cain's dynasty is known as "the sons of men". It culminates in the self-centred boasting of Lamech: *"I have killed a man for wounding me, a young man for injuring me."* Their rage against God turns into rage against anyone who reminds them that the universe does not revolve around them at all.

But Adam and Eve have another son named Seth. His dynasty is known as "the sons of God" because they *"began to call on the name of the Lord."* We are told that Enoch *"walked faithfully with God"* and that Noah *"was a righteous man, blameless among the people of his time, and he walked faithfully with God."* These events happened

---

1 This sacrificial lamb pointed to the death of Jesus on the cross. That's why Jesus in Luke 11:50–51 calls Abel the first prophet, despite the fact that Abel does not speak a single word in the Bible.

many thousands of years ago but they are just as relevant today. Seth's family were the first believers, the first to confess gladly that God is God and we are not. God prized their worship so highly that he gave them a starring role in Part 1 of the Bible's story.

Then, in Genesis 6, something terrible happens: *"The sons of God saw that the daughters of men were beautiful, and they married any of them they chose."* Seth's family stopped worshipping God as dependent creatures and married into Cain's self-assertive family.

"I am going to put an end to all people, for the earth is filled with violence because of them," God told Noah. *"Make yourself an ark."* It seemed like a ridiculous command, an impossible command, but Noah believed God and obeyed. In contrast to the violent self-assertiveness, self-centredness and self-worship of his neighbours, we are told twice that *"Noah did everything just as God commanded him."* Once Noah had built his massive boat, God saved his entire family by ensuring that it floated. Genesis 7:16 reminds us that he is the Saviour God by telling us that *"the Lord shut him in."*

Nowadays many people laugh at the story of Noah and his ark, but to do so ignores the fact that a version of this story appears in the ancient writings of all the world's great cultures – as far back as the Mesopotamian epics of Atrahasis and Gilgamesh and the Ancient Greek story of Deucalion, as far west as the Aztecs of Central America, and as far east as the Aborigines of Australia. It is a historical event which teaches us three vital lessons at the start of the Bible.

First, it shows us that God takes it very seriously when we sin by pretending to be little gods. Second, it warns us that God has set a judgment day for sin. In 2 Peter 3 we are warned us that *"in the last days scoffers will come, scoffing and following their own evil desires. They will say, 'Where is this "coming" Jesus promised? Ever since our ancestors died, everything goes on as it has since the beginning of creation.' But they deliberately forget that long ago by God's word… the world of that time was deluged and destroyed. By the same word the present heavens and earth are reserved for fire, being kept for the day of judgment and destruction of the ungodly."* Third, it assures us that God has made a way for sinful people to be forgiven. Men and women who try to be like God will be destroyed, but God became a carpenter like Noah so that whoever trusts in the blood of Jesus can be saved.

If anybody might have been tempted to get stressed out and over-busy then it was Noah when he led his family out of the ark after the Flood. The whole of human civilization had been destroyed and he was in charge of its reconstruction. He had the mother of all to-do lists. Yet the first thing he did when he stepped out of the ark was absolutely nothing. He resolved to live as God had always intended humans to live. He put down his hammer and his axe and he lifted up his empty hands to God in worship.

We are in desperate need of the message of Genesis 1–11. We belong to one of the most stressed-out and self-centred generations in human history. God invites us at the start of the Bible to make a choice between Adam's fig leaves and God's blood sacrifice, between Cain's hard work and Abel's faith, and between Lamech's pride and Noah's obedience.

Will we act like little gods or will we accept that we are creatures whose happiness is bound up in the fact that God is God and we are not?

PART 2
FAMILY

GENESIS 12–50 AND JOB
2200 BC TO 1805 BC

Things fall apart. They did in Noah's family, anyway. Soon after they left the ark they started acting like the family of Cain. Genesis 1–11 ends with a resurgent human race boasting at the building site of the Tower of Babel: *"Let us build ourselves a city, with a tower that reaches to the heavens, so that we may make a name for ourselves."* God thwarts their plans by dividing them into the different nations of the world, and then he starts looking for a new family to succeed that of Seth and Noah.

God's choice is very surprising, but it also makes perfect sense. He does not look for an impressive founder for his new family. He chooses a complete nobody because zeroes find it easier than heroes to admit that God is God and we are not. This is a particularly important principle if you are reading this book as a non-Christian. Don't be put off by the failings of many Christians. That misses the point. Christians are a bunch of nobodies who are following a great Somebody! Don't go to the opposite extreme and assume that you could never turn to God because your lifestyle is not as virtuous as some of your Christian friends' lifestyles. That misses the point too. God chooses nobodies and he takes responsibility for turning them into the people he created them to be.

Abraham is a complete nobody. He is an idolater. Joshua 24:2 recalls that *"Long ago your ancestors, including Terah the father of Abraham and Nahor, lived beyond the River Euphrates and worshipped other gods."* Abraham worships creatures instead of his Creator. What is more, he is heir to the builders of Babel. He lives in Ur of the Chaldees, the largest city in the world, which was famous for its ziggurat tower and for the fact that its rulers claimed they were gods. He is so thoroughly immersed in Babel's culture that he marries his sister and thinks this also gives him the right to have sex with her slave-girl. Abraham is shameful. You wouldn't want him in your neighbourhood. Yet the Lord chooses him to be the founder of the Family of God.

If you understand a little bit about ancient culture, then you will fathom Abraham's shortcomings even more. Because I am a twenty-first-century Westerner, I love my four children equally – my daughter just as much as my three sons. But the ancient world was a very different place. The firstborn son was everything. A father's other sons and daughters were also-rans. Abraham was about sixty years younger than his older brother. He was an afterthought, a mistake, an absolute nobody.[1] To make things even worse, he was infertile. Whatever else God was looking for in the founder of his new family, the ability to have children was essential. Abraham was childless at the age of seventy-five. Hebrews 11:12 doesn't pull its punches when it tells us that he was *"as good as dead."*

That's the big picture of Part 2 of the Bible. God isn't looking for followers who are brilliant. He is looking for people who admit that they are nobodies and who believe that God is the great Somebody. He is looking for people who are willing to gamble everything on the fact that God is God and they are not.

What Abraham lacks in credentials, he makes up for in faith. He throws out his idols. He waves goodbye to the most civilized city in the world and becomes a nomad, pitching his tent among the hostile inhabitants of Canaan. When God tells him to change his name from Abram to Abraham, he is not simply asking him to add two extra letters to his name. Abraham means *Father-of-Many*, so God is asking the infertile ninety-nine-year-old to declare to his neighbours that he trusts God's promises in spite of their laughter and all the evidence to the contrary.

Genesis 15:6 tells us that *"Abram believed the Lord, and he credited it to him as righteousness."* He gambled everything on the faithfulness of God and he reaped

---

1   Terah became father to Haran aged 70 and father to Abraham aged 130 (Genesis 11:26, 32; 12:4). That's why Haran died long before Abraham and why Abraham treated his nephew, Lot, more like a brother (13:8).

the reward. When he was aged 100, the Lord gave him a son and made him the founder of the Family of God. The life of Abraham reminds us that the kind of faith which marks the members of God's Family is always spelt R-I-S-K.

Abraham's son Isaac is an absolute nobody too. He is not the firstborn, since Abraham has sinfully conceived another child by having sex with his wife's slave-girl. Isaac is a bad husband, allowing the king of the Philistines to take his wife into his harem rather than risking his own neck in order to defend her honour. He is a bad father, provoking his younger son to anger by making it clear that he loves his older son much more.

Nevertheless, Isaac is the kind of person God can use. Despite his many failings, he believes God and risks everything to follow him. We tend to focus on the fact that Isaac is duped into blessing the wrong son with all the promises God made to Abraham, but Hebrews 11:20 focuses on the fact that he blessed his children with those promises at all: *"By faith Isaac blessed Jacob and Esau in regard to their future."* Isaac had many flaws but his heart was full of faith to see the fulfilment of what God had spoken over his family.

When we read Genesis 22, we tend to focus on Abraham's faith in offering Isaac as a sacrifice to God, but the Jewish historian Josephus tells us that this event took place when Isaac was aged 25 and his father was aged 125.[2] When a 25-year-old wrestles with a 125-year-old, there can only be one outcome, so Genesis 22 is as much about Isaac's faith as it is

---

2   Josephus Flavius in his *Antiquities of the Jews* (1.13.2–4).

about his father's. As he climbs Mount Moriah, the hill which has a famous outcrop known as Calvary, he asks his father, *"Where is the lamb for the burnt offering?"* He lies down willingly on the altar because he trusts his father when he replies, *"God himself will provide the lamb for the burnt offering, my son."* God intervenes by providing a sheep to die in Isaac's place, because Jesus would die in our place on that same mountain 2,000 years later.

Don't miss the big picture in the story. God is looking for nobodies who will put their faith in the Gospel and gamble everything to follow him.

Isaac's son Jacob is the biggest nobody of them all. He is not the firstborn son and he is a dishonest schemer. In the earliest written book of the Bible, God praises a non-Hebrew contemporary of Jacob by asking, *"Have you considered my servant Job? There is no one on earth like him; he is blameless and upright, a man who fears God and shuns evil"* (Job 1:8). Jacob is indeed nothing like him. He takes advantage of his blind father, he double-crosses his older brother and he tries to wrestle God into submission instead of bowing down before him.

But Jacob believes God and risks everything to follow him. While Esau asserts himself over creation with his bow and arrows, Jacob meditates on the promises which the Creator God made to his father. The New Testament is astonishingly generous towards Jacob. It tells us that his scheming and his wrestling were acts of flawed but fervent faith. He reaps years of pain and sorrow because he tries to follow God in the wrong way, but he ends his life as gloriously as

Abraham and Isaac. Hebrews 11:21 tells us that *"By faith Jacob, when he was dying, blessed each of Joseph's sons, and worshipped."* God doesn't expect you to be impressive; he simply expects you to respond to his promises with raw faith.

Jacob's son Joseph is a nobody too. He isn't the firstborn; he is the eleventh-born! He is so untactful towards his older brothers when he boasts about his dreams that they fake his death and sell him to slave-traders who are bound for Egypt. Yet Joseph believes God and risks everything to follow him. When his master's wife attempts to seduce him, he asks her, *"How... could I do such a wicked thing and sin against God?"* When she is offended and has him thrown into a dungeon, he does not grow resentful towards God. When Pharaoh's butler and baker have troubled dreams, he does not say, "Don't talk to me about dreams; I had dreams once and look where they landed me!" Instead, he trusts God, even forgiving his brothers by asking them, *"Am I in the place of God? You intended to harm me, but God intended it for good to accomplish what is now being done, the saving of many lives."* Because he trusts God in adversity, Joseph becomes the Egyptian prime minister and saves both his family and the most powerful nation in the world.

Part 2 of the Bible therefore ends by inviting its readers to become part of the Family of God themselves. Joseph tricks his brothers into admitting that they are nobodies who need to believe in God's blood sacrifice and risk everything to follow him.[3] At

---

3   See Genesis 41:16; 42:21–22, 28; 44:16, 32–33. Judah was the ancestor of Jesus, so his willingness to sacrifice his own life for that of Benjamin points towards Jesus' death on the cross for us.

the end of Genesis, Joseph calls them to leave their homes and come to Egypt, re-enacting the same call which God issued to their great-grandfather in Ur of the Chaldees. Whether you consider yourself a Christian or a non-Christian ultimately doesn't matter. What matters is whether you believe enough in God to gamble everything on following him. That's the thing which has always marked the Family of God. It still marks God's Family today.

PART 3
DIFFERENT

EXODUS, LEVITICUS, NUMBERS AND DEUTERONOMY
1805 BC TO 1406 BC

The descendants of Abraham didn't find it easy to live in Egypt. They felt as out of place as a Justin Bieber fan at a Metallica concert. The Egyptians did not like them, refused to eat with them, and eventually enslaved them.

During the four hundred years which pass between the death of Joseph and the Exodus, God's Family of believers becomes a nation of Hebrew slaves.[1] The Israelites discover that God's calling makes them as different from their neighbours as their God is different from their neighbours' idols.

To the casual observer, the Egyptians look stronger than ever at the start of the book of Exodus. In around 1566 BC, a new pharaoh ends centuries of

---

[1] *Exodus* is the Greek word for *exit*. *Leviticus* is Greek for *things relating to the Levites*. *Numbers* is named after the two big censuses of Israel in chapters 1 and 26.

infighting by establishing himself as the first ruler of the Eighteenth Dynasty and of the New Kingdom. He enslaves the Hebrews and uses them as the workforce for a massive wave of civic construction. Egypt becomes a superpower with the world's largest empire and Egypt's gods appear to be the rulers and shapers of world history. But the casual observer completely misses the big picture. Exodus, Leviticus, Numbers and Deuteronomy are the historical record of the early years of the Hebrew nation from God's perspective. These four books declare on every page that Israel's God is different from the idols of the nations, and that those who follow him must become very different too.

In the early chapters of Exodus, God demonstrates that he is far smarter than any of his rivals. When Pharaoh oppresses and enslaves the Hebrews, God uses it to scatter and multiply them throughout the whole of Egypt. When Pharaoh commits genocide against them, God uses it to infiltrate a Hebrew baby into the heart of the Egyptian royal family. Moses becomes the leader of the Hebrews and the author of the Pentateuch,[2] but before God can use him he has to learn the same lesson as his ancestors. When his pride persuades him that he can rescue God's Family from slavery on his own, he enters forty years of exile in the desert, where he learns true humility and faith. By the time God appears to him at the burning bush in Exodus 3 and reveals himself as *Yahweh*, or *the*

---

2   The five books of Moses – Genesis, Exodus, Leviticus, Numbers and Deuteronomy – are collectively known as the Pentateuch. This is simply the Greek word for a *Story-in-Five-Volumes*.

Lord, Moses is fully aware that he is a nobody who needs to believe in his Creator and risk everything to follow him.

This awareness enables Moses to orchestrate the greatest escape story in world history. He makes the long trip back home and enters Pharaoh's throne room to command him to let his Hebrew slaves go. When Pharaoh refuses, Moses unleashes a series of miracles which demonstrate how different Israel's God is from Egypt's idols. The plagues confront, among others, the snake-goddess Wadjet, the Nile-god Hapy, the frog-goddess Heket, the cow-goddess Hathor, and the sun-god Amun-Ra.[3] Finally, God confronts the biggest idol of them all: the hope which the ancient world placed in their firstborn sons. Pharaoh begins the contest by asking in Exodus 5:2, *"Who is the Lord, that I should obey him and let Israel go?"* He ends the contest as a corpse floating face down in the Red Sea along with the rest of his mighty chariot army.

Rescuers do not always want to live with those they rescue. When I rescue spiders from my bathtub, I immediately show them the door or toss them out of the window. But God is different. He is so determined to turn this nation of Hebrews into his Family that he tells them in Exodus 19:4 that *"You yourselves have seen what I did to Egypt, and how I carried you on eagles' wings and **brought you to myself**."* He is

---

3   Exodus 12:12 tells us that the Lord used these ten plagues to demonstrate his vast superiority over any of the false gods in the world. Numbers 33:4 tells us that *"the Lord had brought judgment on their gods."*

more than their Deliverer; he is also their destination. He leads the Hebrews to Mount Sinai and descends to earth in order to set up home at the heart of the Israelite nation. He tells Moses in Exodus 29:45–46 that his great goal in saving them is to *"dwell among the Israelites and be their God... I am the Lord their God, who brought them out of Egypt **so that I might dwell among them.***" This is such an important insight into God's character that Moses prays in Exodus 33:15–16, *"If your Presence does not go with us, do not send us up from here... What else will distinguish me and your people from all the other people on the face of the earth?"* God therefore commands the Israelites to build a special tent called a Tabernacle before they leave Mount Sinai, so that his presence can travel with them all the way to the Promised Land.

If the first half of Exodus contains some of the most exciting chapters in the Bible, then the second half of Exodus and the whole of Leviticus contain some of the dullest. Drama gives way to detail about the Jewish Law, and adventure gives way to the architecture of the Tabernacle. Many readers respond by skim-reading these chapters or by giving up on reading the Pentateuch altogether. But this misses the big picture. These chapters are not a digression or an anticlimax. They emphasize that God is different from pagan idols and that when he moves into the neighbourhood everything must change. The ringing cry of these chapters is found in Leviticus 11:45, where God tells the Hebrews, *"I am the Lord, who brought you up out of Egypt to be your God; therefore be holy, because*

I am holy." Holy means different. God comes to dwell in the Tabernacle and then teaches his People how to be as different from their neighbours as he is from their neighbours' idols.

These four books are full of *blood sacrifice*. They contain more slaughter than the complete works of Quentin Tarantino. We find this repulsive because we like our meat to come from the supermarket in clean packages, but God catalogues this sacrificial slaughter in painstaking detail because he wants us to grasp that *"without the shedding of blood there is no forgiveness"* (Hebrews 9:22). Sin is repulsive, so God does not want us to fool ourselves that the good works of sincere Muslims and Buddhists and Westerners can ever save them. From the moment he commands the Hebrews to kill a Passover lamb and to smear its blood onto the vertical and horizontal wooden doorframes of their houses, God teaches them that sin can only be forgiven through the future death of his Son on a wooden cross. Every time the Israelites slaughtered an animal at the altar in front of their Tabernacle, they expressed the same primitive faith as Abel and Isaac in *"the Lamb of God, who takes away the sin of the world!"* (John 1:29).

These four books are full of *rules*. When God comes to live with people, it affects what they can eat, what they can drink, what they can wear, what they can say and who they can sleep with – every single aspect of their lives. Some people misunderstand the purpose of these rules, as if God is telling us to pull our socks up and try to impress him, but Romans

3:20 tells us this is wrong. The purpose of these rules is to show us just how holy God is and just how sinful we are. They showed the Israelites that they were nobodies who needed to cry out to the God who rescued them from slavery to Pharaoh and ask him to rescue them from slavery to sin as well. God responds six times in Leviticus 20–22 with the same amazing promise: *"I am the Lord, who makes you holy."* God doesn't just command holiness; he provides holiness for anyone who believes.

That's why these four books are full of *God's grace and mercy*. The Lord makes observing the Sabbath one of the Ten Commandments, inviting the Israelites to rest in the fact that he is God and they are not, just as Adam and Eve did in the beginning. He provides them with miraculous food and drink in the desert, and when they start worshipping a golden calf he provides them with forgiveness and a future. When they refuse to show they trust him by risking everything to enter the Promised Land, he protects them for forty years in the desert until their children are old enough to inherit his promises and show that they trust him instead. In the book of Deuteronomy, God renews his covenant with this new generation of Israelites.[4] Any other god would have given up on the rebellious descendants of Abraham many times throughout the story. But God is different and

---

4   *Deuteronomy* comes from a Greek word which means *Repetition-of-the-Law*. The unfaithfulness of the Israelites did not nullify God's faithfulness. If we cannot earn our salvation then we cannot unearn it either!

he promises to make us different too. That's the big picture of Part 3 of the Bible.

PART 4
LAND

JOSHUA, JUDGES AND RUTH
1406 BC TO 1100 BC

Hardly a day goes by without a news story about a patch of land which is only 8,000 square miles in size. It is no bigger than Wales or New Jersey, but the state of Israel dominates the news because its land matters so much to so many people. This can stop us from seeing the big picture when we read Part 4 of the Bible.

Some people struggle with the message of Joshua, Judges and Ruth because they are unimpressed with the actions of the modern state of Israel. They object to the way in which Joshua drives out the indigenous people groups of Canaan in order to settle it with Hebrews. They forget that these events took place almost 3,500 years ago, before the Greeks laid siege to Troy and before the Ancient Britons built Stonehenge. To judge these events based on twenty-first-century priorities is to expect world history to revolve around the thinking of our own generation.

The late Bronze Age was the moment in world history when the human population grew so large that different ethnic groups were forced to fight for the few patches of well-watered land to stay alive. The Hebrews had been enslaved by the Egyptians and repeatedly attacked by the other nations in the region, but God had promised Abraham that he would create a safe haven for them in the Promised Land. These three books of the Bible record how, against all odds, God did as he promised.

Other people struggle to grasp the message of Joshua, Judges and Ruth because they are obsessed with the state of Israel. The subplot of these books is that God gave 8,000 square miles of territory to the Hebrews, which is why the United Nations was right in 1949 to recognize that the Jews have a historic right to live there and that the nation-state of Israel has the right to defend its borders. But if we major on the subplot of these books, then we are in danger of missing the big picture.

The New Testament explains what the books of the Old Testament really mean. Jesus affirmed the importance of the land of Israel by spending most of his earthly life within its borders, but he deliberately undermined the importance of those 8,000 square miles. He took God's ancient promise to the Jews in Psalm 37:11 – *"the meek will inherit the land"* – and he upgraded it in Matthew 5:5 to read: *"Blessed are the meek, for they will inherit **the earth**."* The Jewish rabbi Paul upgraded God's promises to Abraham in a similar way in Romans 4:13. He tells us that *"Abraham and his offspring received the promise that he would be heir* *of the world."* These three books are about far more than 8,000 square miles of Middle Eastern real estate. The Promised Land represents everything which God has promised us through the Gospel.

The Exodus generation missed out on the Promised Land. Ten of the twelve spies they sent to explore Canaan persuaded them to act out of fear instead of faith. *"The land we explored devours those living in it,"* they lied in Numbers 13:32, even as they ate its enormous fruit. They complained that the land was full of massive giants. Hebrews 3–4 warns us that we can miss out on the Promised Land too: *"[Their] bodies fell in the desert... they were not able to enter, because of their unbelief... the message they heard was of no value to them, because those who heard did not combine it with faith... Let us, therefore, make every effort to enter that rest, so that no one will fall by following their example of disobedience."*

Joshua and Caleb were the two spies who encouraged the Israelites to believe God and risk everything to enter the Promised Land, so only they survive to see the start of Part 4 of the Bible. Joshua helps a new generation of Israelites to conquer the land of Canaan from 1406 BC to 1390 BC. The book of Joshua is full of imagery which tells us that God has promised his People something far greater than 8,000 square miles of land.

Joshua and *Jesus* are the same name in Hebrew and in Greek. English Bibles translate them differently to avoid confusion, but God intends us to see Joshua's actions as a prophecy about a better Joshua to come.

Joshua brings victory to the Israelites; Jesus brings victory to the entire world. Joshua sheds the blood of the Israelites through circumcision so that they can enter the Promised Land; Jesus sheds his own blood so that anyone can enter God's Kingdom. Joshua brings down the stronghold of Jericho by commanding the priests to blow on trumpets made from rams' horns; Jesus brings down every stronghold which stands against us because he is the Lamb whose death grants us complete victory.

Joshua saves the life of Rahab, a woman who epitomizes all that is wrong about the sinful Canaanites. She is a liar and a prostitute. She runs a brothel in the walls of Jericho. But she believes in the promises of God and risks everything to follow him, so she and her family are accepted into God's People. She becomes the ancestor of Jesus and a prophetic promise that a day is coming when Jesus will give the work of Joshua a mighty upgrade. Revelation 5:9 worships Jesus because, *"you were slain, and with your blood you purchased for God persons from every tribe and language and people and nation."*

Joshua isn't Jesus. His victory does not last forever. He dies in 1380 BC and Israel is then ruled by fourteen judges. We are told in Judges 2:10–12 that *"After that whole generation had been gathered to their ancestors, another generation grew up who knew neither the Lord nor what he had done for Israel. Then the Israelites did evil in the eyes of the Lord and served the Baals. They forsook the Lord, the God of their ancestors, who had brought them out of Egypt. They followed and worshipped various gods of the*

peoples around them. They aroused the Lord's anger..."
The Israelites started worshipping Baal and the other
idols of the Canaanites whom Joshua drove out of the
land. They forgot their calling to be different from
their neighbours as the Family of God. As a result,
their neighbours came and reoccupied the land.

Part 4 of the Bible asks us to make our own
response to the message of the Bible so far. God
promises us forgiveness and freedom from sin but,
like the judge Samson, we can be blind to how much
we need it. Samson frequented prostitutes and acted
like the family of Cain, so the Philistines captured him
and gouged out his eyes. The truth is, he had blinded
himself to God's big picture long before.

God promises us fruitfulness with the Gospel but,
like the judge Gideon, we can hide away in fear instead
of believing the one who promises us in Psalm 2:8,
*"Ask me, and I will make the nations your inheritance, the
ends of the earth your possession."* The Lord commands
Gideon in Judges 6:14 to *"Go in the strength you have...
Am I not sending you?"* God still commands us with
those same words to go and take our own Promised
Land.

Ruth lived during the rule of the judges, and God
uses her story to provoke us to trust him. She was
a Moabitess, which meant her nation only existed
because Abraham's nephew Lot had a sinful night
of drunken sex with his daughter. This is shameful
enough, but the Moabites were also one of the nations
who tried to annihilate the Hebrews on their way into
the Promised Land.

Ruth is a nobody who is forced to scavenge in the fields with the poorest of the poor, but she believes in the God of Israel and risks everything to become part of his People. She tells her Hebrew relative that *"Where you go I will go, and where you stay I will stay. Your people will be my people and your God my God."* God sees her faith and he saves her. He causes an Israelite named Boaz to fall in love with her, to marry her and to make her a great landowner in Israel alongside him. Together they inherit the promises which God made to Abraham. They become great-grandparents to King David and ancestors to Jesus. They discover that God's Promised Land is far bigger than 8,000 square miles.

God has made you many promises. Part 4 of the Bible asks you what you are going to do with them. Will you shrink back in fear like the Exodus generation, or will you gamble everything on God, like Joshua and Rahab and Ruth and many of the judges?

PART 5
GROW

1&2 SAMUEL, 1 CHRONICLES AND PSALMS
1120 BC TO 970 BC

Healthy things grow. That's just what they do. Healthy plants grow, healthy children grow, healthy friendships grow and healthy people grow spiritually. God doesn't want our lives to be static; he wants them to be great adventures of getting to know him.

If you are not a Christian, then Part 5 of the Bible is for you. It isn't right for you to be asking the same spiritual questions that you were asking five years ago. God wants you to grow in your understanding of him. If you are a Christian, then Part 5 of the Bible is for you too. God doesn't want your relationship with him to be something stagnant, which never deepens from one year to the next. He wants you to grow in him, and he shows you how to do so in these four books of the Bible.

The book of Judges only records the actions of twelve of the fourteen judges of Israel. The start of

1 Samuel tells us about the rule of Eli, the thirteenth judge, and he starts very well. Eli's name is Hebrew for *Going-Up*, so his name boasts that his eyes are fixed on the God of heaven. He is high priest of Israel as well as judge, the man God has appointed to live in the Tabernacle, to offer blood sacrifices on its altar, and to preach the Word of God. If anyone might be able to help the Israelites to grow spiritually, then it is Eli.

Eli did grow but, sadly, 1 Samuel 4:18 tells us he grew fat. Don't be offended if you aren't slim. Part 5 of the Bible isn't about dieting; it is about listening. Eli became a spiritual couch potato, happy to be part of God's People but lacking any real passion to get to know him as his friend. Eli's fatness is meant to be a picture of his complacency. He lazily leaves the work of offering sacrifices to his sons, even though he knows they are sleeping with the worshippers and stealing meat from the altar. He grows fat as a picture of what always happens when we are too lazy or too passive to listen to the Lord.

It is good to express our questions and our honest doubts, but Eli's life reminds us that we should only do so as part of looking for answers and feeding our faith. 1 Samuel 3:1 tells us that *"In those days the word of the Lord was rare; there were not many visions,"* but the problem was not that God had stopped speaking. Eli had stopped listening. When God warned him that his sons were about to die and the Tabernacle was about to be destroyed, he responded passively: *"He is the Lord; let him do what is good in his eyes"* (1 Samuel 3:18). God therefore uses Eli as a warning to couch-potato Christians and non-Christians. Eli died when he fell off a chair and his excessive body weight broke his neck in two.

The fourteenth judge of Israel is everything that Eli should have been but wasn't. Whereas Eli grew fat, Samuel grows strong. He lives up to his Hebrew name, which means either *Hearing-God* or *Heard-By-God*. He grows strong because he is willing to listen to what the Lord has to say. As a young boy, he sleeps inside the Tabernacle and hears God speak to him at night. He replies in 1 Samuel 3:9, *"Speak, Lord, for your servant is listening."* Samuel's willingness to listen is quickly rewarded. We are told a few verses later that *"The Lord... revealed himself to Samuel through his word."*

The Word of God is powerful. It created the universe and now it strengthens Samuel and the nation which he leads. When the Philistines invade the land, Samuel knows precisely what to do. He sacrifices a lamb as an expression of his faith in the one who delivered Abel and Isaac and Moses. Sure enough, the Israelites are strengthened and the Philistines are routed out, but then tragedy strikes. The Israelites reject Samuel as their leader and demand a king. They are not interested in being led by a man whose name means *Hearing-God*. They refuse to wait for the king that God is preparing in the wings to rule when Samuel dies. They declare that they have had enough of listening to God.

Saul becomes king in around 1050 BC. It is a turning point in Israel's history. 1 Samuel 9:2 tells us that Saul was *"as handsome a young man as could be found anywhere in Israel, and he was a head taller than anyone else."* The Bible uses him as another picture of what happens when we fail to listen to the Lord. Whereas Eli grew fat, Saul grew big-headed. His name means *Asked-For* or *Demanded*, and the tragic lesson of his reign is that when we insist on telling God what to do, he often punishes us by giving us what we ask for.

Saul looks strong on the outside but he is feeble on the inside because he never makes room in his life to listen to the voice of God. When David runs away from him, he hides in the Tabernacle because he knows this is the one place that Saul is guaranteed never to go. In 1 Chronicles extra light is shed on the period of history covered by 1 and 2 Samuel, and it tells us that *"Saul died because he was unfaithful to the Lord; he did not keep the word of the Lord and even consulted a medium for guidance, and did not enquire of the Lord. So the Lord put him to death and turned the kingdom over to David."*[1]

The Philistines invade the land once more. They have a giant of a leader in Goliath. By far the tallest man in Israel, Saul is uniquely placed to beat him but, because he has failed to listen to what God has to say, he crumbles at the very moment when he most needs to be strong. He has never stopped to listen, so he is stopped in his tracks by what he sees. That's

---

1   1 Chronicles 10:13–14; 13:3. The Greek name for 1&2 Chronicles means *The-Things-Omitted* because these two books are meant to serve as a supplementary commentary on the events of 1&2 Samuel and 1&2 Kings.

what always happens when we neglect the Bible or the encouragement which God gives us whenever we gather with his People.

Goliath is only defeated because a shepherd-boy named David happens to be delivering cheese to some of the soldiers in Saul's army. There are few jobs less impressive than that of a cheese delivery-boy, but David has been listening to God and his perspective has been transformed. *"Who is this uncircumcised Philistine that he should defy the armies of the living God?"* he fumes (1 Samuel 17:26) before despatching the giant and delivering Israel.

David is to Saul what Samuel was to Eli. He grows strong because he listens to God. His name means *Beloved* and he is the main author of the Psalms, a book which shows us how to have an intimate friendship with the Lord. David is a shepherd-boy, so he reflects in Psalm 23 that *"The Lord is my shepherd, I lack nothing. He makes me lie down in green pastures, he leads me beside quiet waters, he refreshes my soul. He guides me along the right paths... Even though I walk through the darkest valley, I will fear no evil, for you are with me; your rod and your staff, they comfort me... Surely your goodness and love will follow me all the days of my life, and I will dwell in the house of the Lord for ever."* As a result, God rejects Saul and makes David the new king in 1010 BC, declaring that he is *"a man after my own heart; he will do everything I want him to do."*[2]

David meditates on the promises of God, so he knows exactly what to do when he becomes king. Psalm 132 tells us that he looked up from the sheep-

---

2   This is Paul's paraphrase of 1 Samuel 13:14 when he teaches about David in Acts 13:22.

fields of Bethlehem towards the bright lights of the village of Jearim, where the Ark of the Covenant had been left to gather dust during the days of Saul. God had promised to dwell among his People above the Ark of the Covenant, so David *"swore an oath to the Lord, he made a vow to the Mighty One of Jacob: 'I will not enter my house or go to my bed, I will allow no sleep to my eyes or slumber to my eyelids, till I find a place for the Lord, a dwelling for the Mighty One of Jacob'"* (Psalm 132:2–5).

David therefore starts his reign by capturing the city of Jerusalem and erecting a new Tabernacle on the mountain where God provided a sheep to save the life of Isaac. David brings the Ark from Jearim to Jerusalem and he teaches the Israelites how to worship the Lord and listen to his Word. As a result, their nation prospers. They conquer every nation which harassed them during the period of the judges and the reign of Saul. Foreigners come to the Tabernacle in order to worship Israel's God, and David tells his subjects that he is a picture of an even better King who is to come. When we fail to listen to God, we become bigger and bigger in our own eyes, like Eli, and we become big-headed, like Saul. When David discovers that God has made him the ancestor of Jesus, the true and better King of Israel, he whispers in awestruck wonder: *"You have looked on me as a picture of the Man who is on high."*[3]

When did you last say with Samuel, *"Speak, Lord, for your servant is listening"*? When did you last take time to hear God speak to you as he spoke to

---

3   This is a literal translation of the Hebrew phrase which he uses in 1 Chronicles 17:17.

David? If you want to grow spiritually, if you want to become a blessing to those around you, and if you want to strengthen God's People, then it is very easy. You simply need to close your mouth and open your ears. You simply need to let God do the talking.

PART 6
FOLLOW

1&2 KINGS, 2 CHRONICLES, PROVERBS, ECCLESIASTES AND THE SONG OF SONGS
970 BC TO 586 BC

The most requested song at British funerals is Frank Sinatra's "My Way". Here's how it goes:

> I find it all so amusing, to think I did all that.
> And may I say, not in a shy way: "Oh no, oh no,
>   not me; I did it my way"?
> For what is a man? What has he got? If not
>   himself, then he has naught.
> To say the things he truly feels and not the words of
>   one who kneels.
> The record shows I took the blows – and did it my
>   way!

If Part 6 of the Bible had a theme tune, then it would be Frank Sinatra's "My Way". It is the tragic story of the thirty-nine kings who followed David – a record of how they took the blows for trying to do things their own way. For four hundred years, the Lord asked the rulers of Israel to make a choice between following him or trying to forge their own way through life without him. God wants to teach us through their example and to drive their theme tune out of our heads, once and for all, through these six books of the Bible.

King Solomon reigned from 970 BC to 930 BC. His rule could hardly have begun any better. The Lord had promised his father David in 1 Chronicles 17:11–14 that *"when your days are over and you go to be with your ancestors, I will raise up your offspring to succeed you, one of your own sons, and I will establish his kingdom. He is the one who will build a house for me, and I will establish his throne for ever. I will be his father, and he will be my son… I will set him over my house and my kingdom for ever; his throne will be established for ever."*

Solomon fulfils this promise at the start of 1 Kings by asking the Lord to give him such great wisdom that he is able to write the book of Proverbs as a manual for living life God's way and the Song of Songs as a description of marriage when we love each other God's way. Solomon upgrades David's Tabernacle into a magnificent Temple, and he invites the pagan nations to come and worship Israel's God. He becomes a walking advertisement for how much God is willing to bless us if we follow him.

Then, tragedy. Halfway through his reign, Solomon starts to think that he knows better than God. He stops singing the Song of Songs and starts singing along with Frank Sinatra. He fears Egypt's mighty chariot army, so he creates a massive chariot army of his own, despite the fact that God has expressly forbidden him to do so. Not only does this make him rely on his own strength instead of God's strength, but it is also so expensive that he levies unfair taxes on the northern tribes of Israel while sparing his own tribe of Judah. He forges an alliance with Egypt by marrying Pharaoh's daughter, and this move backfires almost immediately when a change of dynasty turns the new pharaoh into a deadly enemy.

Instead of repenting, Solomon forges hundreds more foreign and domestic alliances by recruiting a harem of a thousand wives and concubines. One moment he is tolerating the pagan idols of his foreign wives; the next he is worshipping alongside them.[1] By the time he wakes up from his stupor and writes Ecclesiastes as a frank confession of what he learned through his folly, his reign is almost over. Solomon dies aged only fifty-eight, as a tragic picture of what happens whenever we ignore God's commands and try to do things our way.

Solomon's son Rehoboam succeeds him as king and rules from 930 BC to 913 BC. His reign marks a turning point for Israel. At the start of his reign, he is forced to decide his country's national anthem. Will it be the psalms of David or will it be Frank Sinatra's "My Way"? The leaders of the ten northern tribes threaten to rebel against him unless he stops charging them unfair taxes to support his chariot army, so he seeks advice from the old men who helped his

---

1   1 Kings 3:1–3; 4:7–19, 26; 11:1–13. See Deuteronomy 17:16 and 1 Kings 11:40; 14:25–26.

grandfather David to worship in the Tabernacle and from the young men who helped his father Solomon to run after foreign idols. David's advisers plead with him to obey to God's Word by scrapping the taxes and disbanding the chariot army, but Rehoboam decides to listen to the young men instead. He tells the ten northern tribes in 1 Kings 12:11 that *"My father laid on you a heavy yoke; I will make it even heavier. My father scourged you with whips; I will scourge you with scorpions."* King Solomon had hummed Frank Sinatra's song, but King Rehoboam would sing it from the rooftops. The ten northern tribes rebel against him and Israel is torn in two. We always reap disaster when we refuse to follow God and decide to do things our way.

Nineteen kings from nine dynasties rule the northern kingdom of Israel from 930 BC to 722 BC. Not one of them decides to do things God's way. Frank Sinatra's song becomes the constant national anthem of the ten northern tribes, right from the moment when God makes a junior official of Solomon their first king. The Lord promises Jeroboam in 1 Kings 11:38 that *"If you do whatever I command you and walk in obedience to me and do what is right in my eyes… I will build you a dynasty as enduring as the one I built for David."* But Jeroboam is too afraid to let his subjects travel south across the border to worship the Lord in Jerusalem. He erects two images of God as he imagines him, one in the southern city of Bethel and one in the northern city of Dan, telling the Israelites in 1 Kings 12:28 that *"It is too much for you to go up to Jerusalem. Here are your gods, Israel, who brought you up out of Egypt."*

Many people read 1 and 2 Kings, as well as 2 Chronicles which supplements the message of 1 and 2 Kings, and they are flabbergasted that the Israelites were so obtuse and spiritually suicidal. This completely misses the big picture. We all find it tempting to chisel for ourselves a modified version of the God of the Bible. Those verses about hell? They're a bit medieval; let's get out the chisel. Those verses which say that God reserves sex for one man and one woman within marriage? They're a bit prudish; let's chisel a bit more. Those verses about giving God my money and my time and my obedience? Chisel, chisel, chisel and chisel some more. Part 6 of the Bible warns us what will happen to any of us if we seek to modify God's Word by singing "I'll do it my way."

Nineteen kings from David's dynasty rule the southern kingdom of Judah from 930 BC to 586 BC. Half of them make Frank Sinatra's song their national anthem, even after God uses the Assyrians to destroy the northern kingdom of Israel in 722 BC. The other half decide that they will follow God, but even they find it hard to do so consistently over the long term. King Asa plunders God's Temple to buy help from a pagan ally, so he dies from a severe sickness of the genitals. King Jehoshaphat pursues false unity with the northern kingdom by marrying his son to the daughter of wicked King Ahab and Queen Jezebel. After his death, her bloody bid for power almost wipes out his entire family. Amaziah, Uzziah, Hezekiah and Josiah – even the best kings of Judah start singing Frank Sinatra at times in their old age. When Jerusalem is destroyed by the Babylonians at the end of 2 Kings in 586 BC, no one thinks that God has been unfair. Instead, we are amazed that God was patient for so long.

If you are not a Christian or if you are a new Christian, God wants to speak to you through the kings of Israel. He wants you to grasp that you can never be happy unless you live life God's way. If you are an older Christian, God wants to speak to you through the kings of Judah. He wants you to go the distance in following him because, as any runner can tell you, it's not how you start a race which matters but how you end it. They say about marriage that men leave without saying goodbye, whereas women say goodbye without leaving. The same is true of Christians. Young Christians whose faith grows cold stop going to church, but older Christians whose faith grows cold keep going to church. They just start humming "I'll do it my way" on the inside.

Part 6 of the Bible ends with a reminder that God's promises to David will be fulfilled through the last king of Israel – one who is never mentioned by name in 1 and 2 Kings or in 2 Chronicles, but whose arrival is prophesied on every page. On the night before he was crucified, Jesus prepared himself to wear a crown of thorns by declaring to God the Father in Matthew 26 that the theme tune of his Kingdom would be *"Not what I want, but what you want... May your will be done."*

Jesus calls us to follow him. He calls us to repent of our sin and to tell God that we will never sing "I'll do it my way" ever again. Part 6 of the Bible isn't just a record of ancient history. Jesus summed up its message when he called his disciples to *"Come, follow me."*

PART 7
SIRENS

ISAIAH, JEREMIAH, LAMENTATIONS, EZEKIEL, HOSEA, JOEL, AMOS, OBADIAH, JONAH, MICAH, NAHUM, HABAKKUK AND ZEPHANIAH
760 BC TO 571 BC

Martin Luther changed the map of Europe through his understanding of the Bible. The Reformation wasn't just a Christian revival. What he discovered in his Bible studies still echoes in the thinking of the modern world. Yet even Luther found it difficult to understand the writings of the Old Testament prophets. He complained that *"They have a strange way of talking, like people who, instead of proceeding in an orderly manner, ramble off from one thing to the next, so that you cannot make head or tail of them or see what they are getting at."*[1]

Most readers of the Bible can identify with Martin Luther's frustration. The first seventeen books of

---

1   Martin Luther in his *Works* (volume 19), *Lectures on the Minor Prophets*.

the Old Testament are relatively straightforward to understand. They are history books about events in ancient Israel, and we learn to read history books at school. The next five books of the Old Testament require a bit more effort, but these books of wisdom literature yield a speedy return on our investment. Job, Psalms, Proverbs, Ecclesiastes and the Song of Songs contain some of the best loved and most quoted verses in the entire Bible.

It is the final seventeen books of the Old Testament which we tend to find most difficult to understand. Prophets who lived 2,500 years ago used wild imagery and cryptic poetry to convey messages from God about the past, the present and the future. We are so far removed from the culture into which these prophecies were spoken that we really have to concentrate in order to understand them. But for those who originally received these words, these books of the Bible served as powerful warning sirens that they were missing God's big picture.

The seventeen books of prophecy at the end of the Old Testament represent only a fraction of the prophecies which God inspired during the period. Over a dozen other prophets and prophetesses are mentioned in 1 and 2 Kings and in 2 Chronicles, including famous ones such as Elijah and Elisha, but only seventeen books of prophecy made it into the Old Testament. Two prophets speak primarily to the northern kingdom of Israel (Amos and Hosea), two speak primarily to the Assyrians (Jonah and Nahum) and one speaks primarily to the Edomites (Obadiah).

Eight speak primarily to the southern kingdom of Judah – either before the destruction of Jerusalem (Isaiah, Joel, Micah, Habakkuk and Zephaniah), or in the run-up to its destruction (Jeremiah and Ezekiel), or in order to lament its destruction when it finally came (Lamentations, which was probably written by Jeremiah).[2] But although the thirteen books I have just listed were delivered by very different individuals over a period of two hundred years, they all have one big thing in common. They act as warning sirens which attempt to awaken a world which is spiritually asleep and in terrible danger.

These books of prophecy sound a warning siren that *all is not well*. They were delivered to people who believed that God was happy with their lifestyle and who were certain that the future held nothing for them other than peace and prosperity (Jeremiah 6:14; 8:11). The prophets were willing to pay a hefty price to grab their attention and to warn them that they were wrong.

Hosea marries a prostitute as a symbol of how unfaithful Israel is being towards the Lord. Ezekiel bakes his food over manure and shaves his head as a warning that siege and exile are just around the corner for Jerusalem. Isaiah offends his strict Jewish listeners by telling them that God is no more impressed by their sanctimonious good deeds than he would be if they tried to offer him a used and bloodied sanitary towel.

---

2   Four of the seventeen books of Old Testament prophecy belong to the period after the destruction of Jerusalem (Daniel, Haggai, Zechariah and Malachi), so we will examine the message of those books in Parts 8 and 9 of the story.

Jeremiah speaks so forcefully that his listeners throw him down a well.

God sounds a noisy warning siren because he is about to judge the nations of the Middle East through the destruction which accompanied the creation of the Assyrian and Babylonian Empires. If you find these prophecies excessively long and detailed, then you need to grasp how much God wants to save people instead of judging them. Amos 3:7 assures us that *"the Sovereign Lord does nothing without revealing his plan to his servants the prophets."* These books urge people to repent and receive God's forgiveness before Judgment Day comes.

These books of prophecy sound a warning siren that *we cannot save ourselves.* Isaiah laughs at Judah's deaf and dumb idols, pointing out that a block of wood or a piece of stone cannot save anyone. In case we nod too easily at this frank assessment of ancient idolatry, Ezekiel 14:3 reminds us that it is easier to create an idol in our hearts than it is to chisel one out of wood or stone. England is as full of idols as Israel, and America is as full of idols as Assyria. Our idols are simply on the inside. The prophets warn us that reliance on our money or our cleverness or our friends or our government or our loved ones will always let us down. Jeremiah 2:13 warns us that placing our trust in anything other than God is doubly foolish, because it fails to save while lulling us into a false sense of security which stops us looking to the Lord as Saviour instead.

The Edomites trust in their fortifications to save them. Obadiah tells them that only God can save them from the Babylonian armies. The people of Judah trust in their Temple to save them. Ezekiel tells them that the Lord has abandoned their Temple. (Nobody noticed when his presence left the building, as is still the case in many dying churches today.) Jeremiah tells them it is about to be destroyed like the Tabernacle in the days of Eli. The Assyrians trust in their powerful armies to save them, but Jonah warns them that they are nobodies who will only be saved if they repent and lay down everything to believe in Israel's God. Remarkably, the Assyrians of Nineveh repent while the people of Jerusalem refuse. This forms another great theme of these books of prophecy: the God of Israel promises that he is planning to save people from every language and nation.

These books of prophecy therefore sound a warning siren that *we need to lay hold of God's message of salvation*. They take us back to the Law which Israel received at Mount Sinai in order to help us to confess that we are sinners who deserve God's judgment. They talk about the blood sacrifices in the Temple and they start to explain how they are going to be fulfilled through the coming of God's Messiah. Isaiah tells us that, astonishingly, God is about to become a human being and that, as the true King of Israel, he will succeed where David's sinful dynasty has clearly failed (Isaiah 9:6–7). Isaiah prophesies that this Messiah will be the sacrificial Lamb for whom God's People have been waiting for centuries (53:4–7). He will live a sinless life (53:9), die a sacrificial death (53:8) and be raised to life (53:10–12) in order to save people from every nation

(49:6). These long chapters of prophecy may be gory, offensive and disturbing, but they are never devoid of hope. They spell out how much we need God's mercy, but then they promise us that God extends towards us all the mercy that we need.

The northern kingdom of Israel ignored God's warning sirens. In 722 BC, it was destroyed. The southern kingdom of Judah ignored God's warning sirens. In 586 BC, it was destroyed too. The wailing sound of God's warning sirens still rings out over our own lives through Part 7 of the Bible, and he still uses these books to call us to repent and put our trust in him.

The Lord shouts to us in Isaiah 45:22: *"Turn to me and be saved, all you ends of the earth; for I am God, and there is no other."* He pleads with us to take these warning sirens seriously in Ezekiel 18:31–32: *"Why will you die...? For I take no pleasure in the death of anyone, declares the Sovereign Lord. Repent and live!"*

PART 8
FOREIGN GROUND

DANIEL AND ESTHER
605 BC TO 473 BC

Some people will do anything to get in the *Guinness Book of Records*. Living in London, I really ought to have a go myself. The current record for the number of people who have managed to squeeze into one of London's famous red telephone boxes is sixteen. Next time I have a party at my house, I've half a mind to take my friends down the road so that we can squeeze our way into the record books.

Seventeen people in a red London telephone box may sound ridiculous, but it isn't as ridiculous as what the Jewish nation tried to do in the Old Testament. They tried to squeeze God into a box and, in Part 8 of the Bible, he breaks out of it and demonstrates that the entire world is his. We can be just as guilty of trying to squeeze God into a box today. We expect him to show up at church or at religious gatherings, but we tend not to expect him to turn up at work, at school, or when we are out with certain groups of friends. That's why Daniel and Esther are such important books of the Bible. God saw the Jewish exile in Babylon and Persia as the perfect opportunity to teach his People that, for him, there is no such thing as foreign ground.

Trying to squeeze the Lord of the universe into a box is both ridiculous and insulting. Abraham knew him as the Most High, Moses knew him as the great Deliverer, Joshua knew him as the Conqueror and David wrote in Psalm 24:1 that *"The earth is the Lord's, and everything in it."* Solomon grasped that even his magnificent new Temple could never shut God in, praying in 1 Kings 8:27, *"will God really dwell on earth? The heavens, even the highest heaven, cannot contain you. How much less this temple I have built!"* But somehow the Jews had forgotten this along the way.[1] They assumed that God dwelt above the Ark of the Covenant (a golden box) in the Temple (a bigger box) in Jerusalem (an urban box) in the land of Judah (their national box). So when the Babylonians destroyed the Ark and the Temple and Jerusalem and Judah in 586 BC, the Jews assumed it was game over for God's story. In reality, God was only getting started.

Daniel is still a teenager in 605 BC when he is taken to Babylon as part of the earliest group of Jewish exiles. King Nebuchadnezzar changes his name from Daniel, which was Hebrew for *God-Is-My-Vindicator*, and renames him Belteshazzar, which is Aramaic for *The-*

---

1   There would be no triumphant return for the ten northern tribes of Israel, so from this point in the story the surviving Hebrews are normally referred to as *Jews* – that is, the survivors of *Judah*.

Babylonian-Idol-Bel-Will-Stop-Anything-Bad-Happening-To-The-King. He enrols Daniel in classes which indoctrinate him with the thinking of Babylon and its idols. He steals the golden vessels from God's Temple in Jerusalem and puts them in the temple of his own god. Daniel's Jewish friends start to believe that God's big story has ended in failure, but Daniel is convinced that God really meant it when he prophesied in Isaiah 11:9 that *"the earth will be filled with the knowledge of the Lord as the waters cover the sea."* Daniel does not try to squeeze God into a Jewish box. As a result, he experiences the power of God in Babylon.

We live in a culture which tells students to keep their faith out of the classroom, and which tells workers they are unprofessional if they bring their faith into the office. The first chapter of Daniel shows us how to resist this pressure to compartmentalize our lives.

Daniel is not a troublemaker. He allows King Nebuchadnezzar to rename him and he immerses himself in his pagan studies because he believes that the more he understands the Babylonians, the more he will be able to direct them towards Israel's God. But there comes a point at which he feels the king is compromising his obedience to the Lord. He refuses to eat meat or drink wine which has been offered to the false gods of Babylon. His teacher is aghast and tries to persuade him that such a stand in the workplace is suicidal. But the God who abandoned his Temple in Jerusalem performs a miracle for Daniel in Babylon. He will do the same for you if you refuse to lie, neglect church gatherings or compromise your faith in any way for the sake of your career. God shows he is as interested in our work life as he is in our leisure time by vindicating Daniel so that he is promoted to a senior position in the government of Babylon.

Daniel's official duties have taken him elsewhere in the empire when King Nebuchadnezzar tries to intimidate the Jews in Babylon again. Three of Daniel's friends defy the king's command to worship a golden idol, and they are thrown into a fiery furnace. We can imagine the fine-sounding arguments of the Jewish friends who tried to save their lives. They were causing trouble for the Jewish race as a whole. They had lost their land and the box which housed their God, so what were they thinking by expecting God to show up and protect them on foreign ground? Yet Nebuchadnezzar looks into the fiery furnace and exclaims, *"Weren't there three men that we tied up and threw into the fire?... Look! I see four men walking around in the fire, unbound and unharmed, and the fourth looks like a son of the gods"* (Daniel 3:24–25).

The other Old Testament prophets talk about the Messiah, but Daniel's friends actually see him. He comes down to earth early in order to stand shoulder to shoulder with them when they gamble everything on their belief that God is with them. Nebuchadnezzar, the man who led the armies which destroyed Jerusalem and its Temple, is so impressed that he proclaims that Israel's God is greater than his idols. God breaks out of the Jewish box and brings salvation to the very heart of Babylon.

Politicians have a bad name. Many Christians ape the cynicism of their neighbours and leave the task of governing nations and communities and schools to other people. That's why it's so significant that Daniel and his friends roll up their sleeves and take senior positions in the government of the Babylonian Empire. Daniel gets close enough to Nebuchadnezzar to interpret his dreams and to tell him that his empire is doomed. As a result, on the very night that Babylon falls to the Persians, the Queen Mother tells the last king of Babylon to turn to Daniel in his hour of crisis: *"There is a man in your kingdom who has the spirit of the holy gods in him. In the time of your father he was found to have insight and intelligence and wisdom like that of the gods... Call for Daniel"* (Daniel 5:11–12).

As a result, Daniel becomes one of the leading rulers of the Persian Empire, which gives him an opportunity to proclaim God's power to another group of nations. When King Darius forbids him to pray to the Lord for thirty days, Daniel refuses and is thrown into a den of lions. It is now 538 BC and Daniel is in his eighties, but he gambles one last time on the fact that God is with him. The king of Persia is so impressed by his survival that he issues a decree, *"that in every part of my kingdom people must fear and reverence the God of Daniel. For he is the living God and he endures for ever"* (Daniel 6:26).

You may be tempted to put God in a box and leave him out of your workplace or your studies. You may be tempted to assume he isn't interested in politics or in helping you to make a difference in your community. If so, you need to learn from the Dutch pastor Abraham Kuyper who left church leadership to become prime minister of the Netherlands. He explained, *"There is not a square inch in the whole domain of our human existence over which Christ, who is Sovereign over all, does not cry: 'Mine!'"*[2] If your biggest temptation is to leave God out of conversations with your family and friends, acting differently with certain groups of people, then the book of Esther is for you.

Anyone who has watched the movie *300* knows that King Xerxes of Persia was one of the bad guys. He was the enemy of Leonidas and his 300 Spartans. The book of Esther begins with the great party which he threw in 483 BC for his commanders before they set out to invade Greece. Xerxes gets drunk and decides to summon his beautiful wife so that his friends can ogle her body. When she refuses, Xerxes immediately banishes her. However far away from God your friends may seem, they are not as far away from him as was King Xerxes of Persia.

When he returns home from defeat in Greece, Xerxes decides that he must find himself a new trophy wife. He creates a harem of the most beautiful women in his empire. One of them is a Jewish girl named Esther, and the king is so taken with her beauty that he declares her the new official queen. When she discovers a plot to annihilate the Jews, she is forced to choose between keeping her head down for the sake of her marriage or blowing her cover as a believer for

---

2   Kuyper was Dutch prime minister from 1901 to 1905. He said this in his inaugural address at the opening of the Free University of Amsterdam in 1880.

the sake of her nation. Her cousin asks her forcefully: *"who knows but that you have come to your royal position for such a time as this?"* (Esther 4:14).

Her cousin asks us the same question as we read Part 8 of the Bible. Wherever we live, wherever we work, wherever we study and wherever we have friends and family – that is the place where God has put us in order to demonstrate his power. There is no foreign ground for God, because he will no more fit inside our boxes than he fitted inside the Jewish one. Let's be like Esther, who not only saved the Jewish race but also brought salvation to the nations of the world. Esther 8:17 tells us that *"there was joy and gladness among the Jews, with feasting and celebrating. And many people of other nationalities became Jews."*

PART 9
DISAPPOINTMENT

EZRA, NEHEMIAH, HAGGAI, ZECHARIAH AND MALACHI
538 BC TO 432 BC

God doesn't always do things our way. If you haven't worked that out yet, then I am sorry to be the bearer of bad news. God is God and we are not, which means he does things his way even when it confuses, frustrates and disappoints us. Following God is incredibly exciting, but it is called a walk of faith for a reason. God is honest about this in Part 9 of the Bible. This final part of the Old Testament is a massive disappointment.

It might have been easier for the Jews if things had not started out so well. In 538 BC, Daniel reads the words of Jeremiah 25 and 29, and he discovers that God prophesies that the Jewish exile will only last for seventy years (Daniel 9). He does some quick sums in his head and calculates that, since he was taken to Babylon in 605 BC, there are only three years left to run before a miracle of deliverance. He starts fasting and praying and, at the start of Ezra, his prayers are immediately answered. King Cyrus of Persia decides that it is time for him to send the Jewish exiles home.

The first four chapters of the book of Ezra are incredibly exciting. The Babylonians had wiped out much of David's dynasty and much of the family from which the high priests were always chosen. King Cyrus reverses their policy by seeking out Zerubbabel, heir to the throne of David, and by appointing him governor of Judah. This is the Old Testament equivalent of the moment in *The Lord of the Rings* when the ranger Strider is suddenly revealed to be Aragorn son of Arathorn. God's big Jewish story gets back underway and, what is more, King Cyrus tracks down Joshua, who is heir to the high priesthood, and appoints him to lead alongside Zerubbabel. Together, they lead over 40,000 Jews back to the Promised Land and start rebuilding the Temple. King Cyrus not only returns the golden vessels which the Babylonians stole from the Temple; he also pays for the building work out of Persian funds! This is what the Jews have been waiting for. They finally feel they are experiencing the God of the Bible.

They lay the foundations for the Temple and rebuild its altar so that they can start offering blood sacrifices to God again. Everything is going well when disaster suddenly strikes. The Samaritans who have settled in the land while the Jews were away lodge a formal complaint to King Cyrus. The Persians call a halt to the rebuilding in 535 BC and the Jews are forced to wait for another fifteen years.

Delay is one of the hardest forms of disappointment to bear. But following God, by definition, means being willing to travel at his speed. We learn in the first four chapters of Ezra how to handle God's delays. First, we need to ask ourselves whether we have perhaps misunderstood the voice of God. Daniel had made the mistake of assuming that God's plans revolved around himself. He had been taken to Babylon in 605 BC, but the destruction of Jerusalem had not taken place until 586 BC. Sure enough, in the second half of Ezra the Temple is completed in 516 BC, exactly seventy years after its destruction.

Second, we need to ask ourselves what God is trying to say to us through delays. We tend to focus on reaching the destination, whereas God wants to enjoy the journey with us and to use it as a chance to shape our character. Two of the last books of the Old Testament record the words which the prophets Haggai and Zechariah spoke to the Jews during this period of waiting. They help us to see what God wants to do in our hearts through disappointment and delay.

Haggai and Zechariah teach us that, when we put our faith in human leaders, they will always let us down. When we ask people to play God for us, we cannot blame them when they fail. When Barack Obama became the first black president of the United States in January 2009, public expectations were so high that the British newspaper *The Times* ran a cartoon of the fountain in front of the White House with a sign which read *"No walking on the water"*. Whenever we turn men into messiahs, they let us down. God uses disappointment in our leaders to lift up our eyes towards Jesus the true Messiah.

The high priest Joshua is a disappointment. He is too sinful for the job. Zechariah sees a vision of him dressed in filthy clothes, but God clothes him in robes of purity and tells him: *"Listen, High Priest Joshua, you and your associates… are men symbolic of things to come: I am going to bring my servant, the Branch… and I will remove the sin of this land in a single day."* God allows the Jews to be disappointed by Joshua in order to make them long for Jesus as the true and better High Priest who is about to come.

Zerubbabel is a bit of a disappointment too. He is too weak to intercede with King Cyrus and he cannot overcome the barriers to rebuilding the Temple. He is not strong enough to fulfil the promises which God has made to Israel. Zechariah prophesies that this is all part of the plan: *"This is the word of the Lord to Zerubbabel: 'Not by might nor by power, but by my Spirit,' says the Lord Almighty."* He promises that the coming Messiah will be King as well as High Priest of Israel. He will be a better Zerubbabel as well as a better Joshua.[1]

The Temple is also a disappointment. While the young Jews rejoice that it is being built at all, the older Jews remember Solomon's Temple and start weeping (Ezra 3:12). It is too small to fulfil what was prophesied

---

1   Haggai and Zechariah prophesied from 520 BC to 518 BC. The verses referred to in this chapter can be found in Zechariah 3:1–10; 4:6; 6:9–15, in Haggai 2:9, in Nehemiah 1:1–4; 13:25 and in Malachi 3:1.

in Ezekiel 40–46, and the Ark of the Covenant has been destroyed. Haggai reassures them, *"The glory of this present temple will be greater than the glory of the former temple"*(Haggai 2:9). Jesus would come to this Temple and in its courtyards he would found the Church as a better Temple. If we had better leaders then we would rely on them instead of Jesus. God loves us so much that he allows them to disappoint us in order to make us look up into the eyes of Jesus.

Some of our bitterest disappointments come when we are let down by our friends. The book of Nehemiah begins in 446 BC, so seventy years pass from the destruction of Jerusalem to the rededication of the Temple, and another seventy years pass from the rededication of the Temple to the rebuilding of Jerusalem's walls. Nehemiah is a Jew who has stayed on in Persia as an important royal official because he trusts his friends to serve God without him in Jerusalem. The book begins with tragic news: *"while I was in the citadel of Susa, Hanani, one of my brothers, came from Judah… They said to me, 'Those who survived the exile and are back in the province are in great trouble and disgrace. The wall of Jerusalem is broken down, and its gates have been burned with fire.' When I heard these things, I sat down and wept. For some days I mourned and fasted and prayed."* If you have ever been let down by your friends, by your neighbours or by your church, then the book of Nehemiah is for you.

Nehemiah takes ownership of the problem and manages to rebuild the walls of Jerusalem in only fifty-two days. The Jewish noblemen let him down by refusing to get their hands dirty, and they let him down a second time by lending money at such high interest rates that the poorest Jews are forced to become their slaves. Nehemiah is furious and he helps the Jews to make a solemn pledge to serve the Lord before he goes back to his work in the Persian capital.

Nehemiah 13 is the last chapter, chronologically, of the Old Testament, and it ends Part 9 on yet another note of disappointment. When he returns to Jerusalem in 432 BC, Nehemiah discovers that the high priest is renting out parts of the Temple to get some extra spending money, that the ordinary Jews are working on the Sabbath and withholding offerings from God, and that they have married pagan idolaters. Nehemiah is so frustrated that he confesses, *"I rebuked them and called curses down on them. I beat some of the men and pulled out their hair"*!

God has to send Malachi, the final prophet of the Old Testament, that same year to focus Nehemiah's eyes on Jesus. Malachi promises that *"suddenly the Lord you are seeking will come to his temple; the messenger of the covenant, whom you desire, will come."* Good friends can easily become idols. It is only when they let us down that we look to Jesus as the friend who sticks closer than any brother.

We have reached the end of the Old Testament. Four hundred years of silence pass between the end of the Old Testament and the beginning of the New. During this period, the Jewish homeland is invaded by Alexander the Great, then by the Seleucids and then finally by the Romans. God remains silent throughout, removing all the background noise so that the Jews can focus on the big picture of the Old Testament. Oswald Chambers suggests that *"If God has given you a silence, then praise Him – He is bringing you into the mainstream of His purposes."*[2] If you feel disappointed with God because he seems not to be speaking to you, then this is good advice. He has stopped talking because he wants to focus your eyes on the big picture of his story.

So if your hopes have been delayed, if your leaders have disappointed you, if your friends have let you down or if God has stopped speaking, don't get bitter. God wants you to enjoy the journey with him as he takes you to the right destination at precisely the right speed. Whenever things around you fail to go according to your plans, he wants to redirect your gaze and make you look into the eyes of Jesus the Messiah.

2   Oswald Chambers in *My Utmost for His Highest* (1924), entry for 11th October.

PART 10
REAL

MATTHEW, MARK, LUKE AND JOHN
6 BC TO 30 AD

Most people grasp that Jesus is the greatest person in the Bible. They treat him like the star football player in a team of downright amateurs. They are right, but they are not right enough. The Bible without Jesus would not be like a football match without football's greatest player. It would be like a football match without a football, without any goalposts and without any football field. Jesus isn't just the only A-list hero in the Bible. He is its entire A to Z. That's why Part 10 of the Bible consists of the same story told four times over. The four different gospels reflect on the importance of the earthly life of Jesus from four different perspectives.

Jesus told his enemies that they had not grasped the big picture of the Old Testament unless they understood that each of its 929 chapters pointed towards the day when he would come to earth as

God's Messiah. He told them in John 5:39 that *"These are the very Scriptures that testify about me."* He said the same thing to his followers after his resurrection in Luke 24:27, 44–45: *"beginning with Moses and all the Prophets, he explained to them what was said in all the Scriptures concerning himself... 'everything must be fulfilled that is written about me in the Law of Moses, the Prophets and the Psalms.' Then he opened their minds so they could understand the Scriptures."* Each part of God's great story is important, but none is more essential than this one. That's why the New Testament begins with four gospels which tell us the story of Jesus over and over again four times.

Matthew was a Jewish tax collector who became one of Jesus' original twelve disciples. He writes his gospel from a Jewish perspective, telling us that Jesus is the *real Israel* who succeeds wherever the Hebrew nation failed. He is the true and better Adam, who prays in a garden and obeys perfectly where Adam disobeyed (Matthew 26:36–39). He is the true and better Israel, who comes up out of Egypt and obeys God in the desert for forty days where Israel failed for forty years (2:15 and 4:1–11).[1] He is the true and better Moses, who promises in his Sermon on the Mount that he has come down from heaven to fulfil the Law of Sinai.

Many non-Jewish readers miss the big picture in Matthew's gospel. They assume that these things

---

1   Matthew's quotation from Hosea 11:1 makes no sense unless we understand that he deliberately presents Jesus to his Jewish readers as the *real Israel*.

are unimportant for Gentiles like themselves. But this is tragic. God wants us to understand that our salvation depends as much on Jesus' perfect life as it does on his sacrificial death. God does not simply forgive us because we believe that all our sins have been counted as if they belong to Jesus; he forgives us because we believe that Jesus' perfect life has been counted as our own. Forgiveness comes through faith, but it comes through faith in the one who obeyed the Law of Moses in every way and who has handed us his spotless track record of obeying God. When God speaks over Jesus, *"This is my Son, whom I love; with him I am well pleased,"* he is telling us how he views anybody who is justified through the perfect life of his Son (Matthew 3:17).

Matthew tells us that Jesus is the real *King of Israel*. He tells us ten times that Jesus is the Son of David, the heir to David's throne, whose coming was prophesied throughout the Old Testament. Unlike the sinful kings of Israel and Judah, Jesus never once sings along with Frank Sinatra. He never decides to do things his own way. Matthew ends his gospel with Jesus sending the subjects of his Kingdom out into the world in order to inherit the promises which God made to Israel in the Psalms.[2]

Mark writes his gospel from a Roman perspective and he tells us that Jesus is the *real Man*. Although John Mark was a Jew who drew much

---

2   Compare Matthew 28:18–20 with Psalm 2:6–8. The Church is the true and better army which was foreshadowed by King David's army in 1 Chronicles 11–12.

of his knowledge about the life of Jesus from the preaching of Peter, both his name and his choice of words betray his Roman thinking. His Hebrew name was John but his gospel is known by his Roman name Mark, and it is full of Latin words imported into the Greek language. He presents Jesus as the real man who is what every red-blooded male in the Roman Empire longed to be, but failed. Mark is the shortest of the gospels, but reading it can be exhausting. He uses very vivid language and one of his favourite words means *suddenly* or *straightaway*.[3] Jesus never stops confronting demons and sicknesses and storms and hypocrites and death. He is stronger than the Roman hero Hercules and more unstoppable than the Roman general Julius Caesar, yet he has not been infected with any of the pride which caused them to fail. He tells us in Mark 10:45 that *"the Son of Man did not come to be served, but to serve, and to give his life as a ransom for many."*

Luke is the only non-Jewish writer of the New Testament. He is an educated doctor from Antioch and he is fascinated by what the life of Jesus means to every single Greek and barbarian. He tells us that Jesus is the *real Saviour*, the only one who can reconcile to God people from every nation. Alexander the Great claimed to be the saviour of the world and so did the Seleucids and the Romans, but Jesus succeeds where all those false saviours failed. Luke sounds just like one of the imperial heralds who took

---

3   He uses the Greek word for *immediately* forty-two times in just sixteen chapters.

news across the Roman Empire when he tells us that the angel declared to the shepherds, *"I bring you good news that will cause great joy for all the people. Today in the town of David a Saviour has been born to you; he is the Messiah, the Lord."*[4]

The word "gospel" means "good news". If somebody discovered a cure for cancer or for HIV, then they would have a gospel message for the entire world. Luke is so excited because Jesus brings the cure for human sin, whether those sins have been committed by Jews or Greeks or barbarians. He brings the Gospel with a capital "G". Instead of tracing the family tree of Jesus back to Abraham, like Matthew, Luke traces it the whole way back to Adam (Luke 3:23–38) and tells us that Jesus came to earth to regain for the entire human race everything which Adam lost in the Garden of Eden (19:10). As a doctor, Luke backs up this claim by recording more examples of Jesus healing the sick and raising the dead than any other gospel writer. He ends his gospel with Jesus' triumphant promise that *"repentance for the forgiveness of sins will be preached in his name to all nations."*

John was one of Jesus' original twelve disciples, and he wrote his gospel later than the other three. He completes their message by emphasizing that Jesus is the *real God*. He deliberately echoes the first verse of Genesis when he starts his gospel by telling us that *"In the beginning was the Word, and the Word was with God, and the Word was God."* Then he takes us on a

---

4   Luke 2:10–11. He particularly emphasizes that Jesus is the Saviour of all nations in Luke 2:29–32; 6:17; 7:9; 10:13–14; 11:29–32; 13:28–30; 17:18; 24:47.

journey through the Old Testament which celebrates the fact that, in Jesus, the God of the Old Testament has become a man.

John tells us that Abraham knew Jesus as Yahweh (John 8:58). He tells us that Moses saw Jesus on Mount Sinai and wrote about him (5:46). He tells us that the prophet Isaiah saw Jesus' glory when he encountered the Lord in the Temple (12:41), and that all the other prophets wrote about him too (1:45). He tells us that Jacob saw a picture of Jesus when he dreamed of a ladder which connected the God of heaven to the human race below (1:51). Jesus is the true Lamb who saved Isaac (8:56), the true Lamb who saved Israel at the Passover, and the true Lamb who was sacrificed in their Tabernacle and Temple (1:29). There is a reason why Jesus is the A to Z of God's great story. He isn't just the star player of human history. He is also the divine writer and director of the entire show.

So take a pause as you consider Part 10 of God's great story and let the four gospel writers help you to see the big picture. Jesus is the real Israel. He is the real King. He is the real Man. He is the real Saviour. He is the real God. He is everything we need.

The four gospels tell us that, first and foremost, the Bible is not about us. Don't miss the big picture. It is all about Jesus.

PART 11
CROSSROADS

MATTHEW, MARK, LUKE AND JOHN
APRIL, 30 AD

World history is full of defining moments: the invention of the wheel, the fall of Rome, the arrival of the hordes of Genghis Khan, the European discovery of America, the invention of the printing press, the discovery of vaccination and penicillin, the first use of the atomic bomb, the dawn of the internet... The list goes on and on.

But all of these defining moments put together have not affected the history of humanity as much as the events which took place across three days in April 30 AD. The symbol of Christianity is not a manger but a cross, because Jesus' cross is the crossroads of history. Jesus was nailed to a wooden scaffold outside Jerusalem and hung from his hands and feet until he died. His corpse was buried but, three days later, he reappeared to his friends alive. The final chapters of each of the four gospels form Part 11 of the Bible.

Jesus dies and is raised to life. The human race will never be the same again.

In the Andrew Lloyd Webber musical *Jesus Christ, Superstar* Judas Iscariot sings to Jesus: *"Did you mean to die like that? Was that a mistake or did you know your messy death would be a record-breaker? Don't you get me wrong – I only wanna know."* Part 11 of the Bible answers this question. It shows us why the death and resurrection of Jesus mark such a massive crossroads in world history: they offer us forgiveness and freedom and a future. Then Part 11 invites us to stand at the crossroads of our own lives and decide how we are going to respond to this Gospel.

The final chapters of the four gospels tell us that Jesus' death and resurrection provide us with forgiveness for our sins. His death was not a mistake. Far from it. It was the very reason why God came to earth in order to live as a man. On the night before his crucifixion, Jesus taught his disciples about *"my blood of the covenant, which is poured out for many for the forgiveness of sins,"* and he told them not to resist his arrest because *"how then would the Scriptures be fulfilled that say it must happen in this way?"*[1] We are not very good at admitting that we need forgiveness. We are one of the most self-justifying generations in human history. But the Bible's message certainly resonates when it talks about guilty consciences and fear of punishment and the sense that God seems very far away. Jesus died and rose again to take away our guilt and to bring us back to God.

1   The verses quoted in this chapter can be found in Matthew 26:28, 54; 27:46; Luke 23:34, 39–43; John 16:11; 19:11, 30.

When Jesus dies on the cross, he is the Lamb of God whose blood was prophesied by Abel and Abraham and Moses and David and Solomon and Isaiah. He is completely sinless but he bears the punishment for our sin in his own body, sucking the serpent venom of the Devil out of our veins and into his. He experiences the judgment we deserve and the horrific abandonment which anyone who rejects his sacrifice will experience in hell. *"My God, my God, why have you forsaken me?"* he cries in agony before answering his own question. *"Father, forgive them,"* he prays, even as he dies.

The Christian writer John Stott explains the significance of Jesus dying in our place for sin: *"The essence of sin is man's substituting himself for God, while the essence of salvation is God substituting himself for man. Man asserts himself against God and puts himself where only God deserves to be; God sacrifices himself for man and puts himself where only man deserves to be. Man claims prerogatives which belong to God alone; God accepts penalties which belong to man alone."*[2] God has gone to the heart of the human problem. He has made a way to bring his sinful creatures home.

The final chapters of the four gospels also tell us that Jesus' death and resurrection provide us with freedom from our sins. Sin doesn't merely pollute our hearts and separate us from God. It is also strangely addictive. When we decide to change our lifestyle, we soon discover that we can't. Jesus deliberately surrendered his power when he died on the cross. He remained silent before his accusers, knowing that he could easily run rings around their testimony and

---

2   John Stott in *The Cross of Christ* (1986).

walk free. He let his creatures crucify him because the nails which pinned him to the cross spoke of the weakness which he bore for us so that he could make us strong. *"You would have no power over me if it were not given to you from above,"* he told the Roman governor who sentenced him. But that's why the death and resurrection of Jesus is such good news. It has channelled God's power towards us so that we can break free from the sins which pin us down. As Jesus dies, he cries out in triumph, *"It is finished!"*

Jesus' death and resurrection also provide us with freedom from shame. None of us wants the world to know who we really are inside. We all have thoughts and feelings and motivations which make us feel ashamed. When I was younger, I used to keep a diary which nobody read except for me. Even so, I did not write down all of my thoughts in my diary. There were certain things I did not even want my future self to know about me.

God knows all of our thoughts, so the gulf between us is not just one of guilt but also one of shame. Jesus dealt with this when he was stripped naked and hung on a cross for all the world to see. For the six hours that he hung there, his ears were filled with the mocking laughter of the crowd. He was crucified outside the city walls of Jerusalem as a picture of our exclusion from heaven. He was crucified between two robbers – yet another mark of shame – but when one of them turned to him for mercy, Jesus did not turn him away. Part 11 of the Bible shows us how completely the death of Jesus has dealt with our shame, when Jesus promises the robber that even a dirty rotten scoundrel like him can now be admitted into heaven.

Jesus' death and resurrection also provide us with freedom from fear. In the ancient world, people were very afraid of demons and magic. While that is still true in much of the developing world, most Westerners tend to be afraid of other things today, such as cancer and sickness and bad luck. Jesus taught that these secular fears are just as much part of the power which the Devil has gained over our lives through human sin. The cross and empty tomb have won back all that Adam lost, which is why Matthew 8:16–17 tells us that Jesus *"drove out the spirits with a word and healed all who were ill. This was to fulfil what was spoken through the prophet Isaiah: 'He took up our infirmities and bore our diseases.'"* Jesus rejoiced over this thought as he prepared himself to die, telling his disciples just before his arrest that *"the prince of this world now stands condemned."*

Jesus' death and resurrection also provide us with freedom from uncertainty. The Gospel is not just a philosophical concept, like Zen Buddhism or atheism. These four books of the Bible are littered with dates, rulers, places and corroborating evidence to back up everything they say. The resurrection is the definitive historical act of proof that God is God and that Jesus is the only Saviour. The facts behind the resurrection testify that the Gospel is true and that any religious or secular viewpoint which denies it is a lie. Instead of wishing that we had greater faith in the Gospel, we simply need to fix our eyes on these historical events. God grants us greater faith even as we do so.

The Oxford professor Géza Vermes weighs the historical evidence for the resurrection and concludes that *"When every argument has been considered and weighed, the only conclusion acceptable to the historian must be that the opinions of the orthodox, the liberal sympathiser and the critical agnostic alike – and even perhaps of the disciples themselves – are simply interpretations of the one disconcerting fact: namely that the women who set out to pay their last respects to Jesus found to their consternation, not a body, but an empty tomb."*[3] This fact freed the early believers from uncertainty and convinced them that God had endued their lives with colossal meaning. They had a job to do, a world to reach, a Kingdom to extend, and a human race to heal and save. Fishermen became apostles, and tax collectors became bestselling authors. That's what can happen when God frees us from uncertainty.

The final chapters of the four gospels tell us that Jesus' death and resurrection provide us with a glorious future. We long for a world without injustice and poverty and bloodshed because we know, deep down, that we were created for such a world. We are like caterpillars who find themselves longing to fly like butterflies, and Part 11 of the Bible tells us that the tomb of Jesus is humanity's cocoon. Jesus comes back to life but his disciples notice that there is something very different about him. He can walk through walls. He can appear and disappear. It is as if he already belongs to another world. We discover in the rest of the Bible that this is because he really does. He is the pioneer of

---

3   Géza Vermes in *Jesus the Jew: A Historian's Reading of the Gospels* (1973).

God's new creation which he will orchestrate when he returns to end world history and to usher in the new eternal age. Those who surrender their lives to Jesus will live forever with him in a paradise which is even more beautiful than the Garden of Eden.

Part of this glorious future is the fact that Jesus' death and resurrection provide us with a future without death. The greatest enemy in our lives is death, but Jesus ate death for his breakfast on Easter Sunday morning. Since death could not hold onto Jesus in the face of God's resurrecting power, its hold over the human race was broken once and for all. Jesus is able to tell the dying thief that, when his body expires, his soul will instantly be transported to God in heaven. The apparent strangeness of Jesus' resurrection body in the final chapters of the gospels acts as a promise that he will also provide new resurrection bodies for us all.

Jesus achieved all of this in only three days. His death and resurrection was by far the most defining moment in human history. His cross still acts as a crossroads, where every person has to choose in which direction they are going to travel: in the way of sinful Adam, or in the way of God's Deliverer.

I encourage you to put down this chapter and to take time to decide what your own response to Jesus' death and resurrection is going to be. He offers you three things: forgiveness and freedom and a future. But he requires of you three things too. He asks you to *admit* you are a sinful nobody who needs a Saviour. He asks you to *believe* his death and resurrection have provided all of the salvation which you need. He asks you to *commit* your life to him, gambling everything on the one who transformed history through his bloodied cross and empty tomb.

This is not my decision. It can only be yours. Tell God that you want to become part of his great salvation story.

PART 12
NEW LIFE

ACTS 1–9
30 AD TO 37 AD

Forty days after his resurrection, Jesus ascended back to heaven. Unless we see the big picture of God's great story, that sounds like terrible news. The whole of human history had been building up to the triumphant moment when God came to earth as a man, but now he had gone back again to heaven. The disciples felt so bereaved by Jesus' ascension that a pair of angels had to ask them: *"Men of Galilee, why do you stand here looking into the sky?"* Another angel had to tell them to *"Go, stand in the temple courts and tell the people the full message of this new life."*[1] The message of Jesus' death and resurrection was not simply to be sung about in churches. It was to be lived and enjoyed and proclaimed throughout the world.

Luke wrote the book of Acts as a sequel to his gospel. He was one of the main leaders of the Early

1   The verses quoted in this chapter are Acts 1:11; 2:47; 3:6; 4:13, 23–31, 34; 5:16, 20, 29, 42; 7:60; 9:2.

Church, so he had a ringside seat on much of what happened in the thirty years after Jesus' ascension to heaven. He expects us to understand the big picture of God's great story and to grasp that the new life which Jesus has provided through his death and resurrection is the fulfilment of everything which has been promised so far in the story. At the start of Acts, the eleven disciples appoint a replacement for the traitor Judas. These twelve disciples are like the founders of the twelve tribes of Israel, re-establishing God's People in the light of the coming of his Messiah.[2] The new life which Jesus has given them enables them to succeed wherever Joseph and his brothers failed.

The early Christians live out Part 1 of the Bible. They experience the same intimate friendship with God which Adam and Eve enjoyed in the Garden of Eden. Adam and Eve sinned and were banished from the tree of life, but Jesus has turned his cross into a new tree of life for his followers. When Jesus promised that God would fill his followers with the Holy Spirit and become their closest friend, he referred to it as *"the promise"* of the Old Testament.[3] When it finally happens on the Day of Pentecost, ten days after his ascension, the early Christians are transformed by the fact that God now lives inside them. They pray powerful prayers, they prophesy with astonishing accuracy, and they walk so closely with the Lord that

2   The New Testament makes it clear that the Church has not replaced the Jewish nation. It is the continuation of the Jewish story, even though many non-Jews are now also included in the story.

3   Luke's Greek phrase is lost in some English translations, but Jesus calls it *"the promise"* in Acts 1:4 and Peter calls it *"the promise"* in Acts 2:39. Being filled with the Holy Spirit is an essential aspect of God's great story.

even their enemies *"were astonished and... took note that these men had been with Jesus."* The early Christians are so full of the Holy Spirit that they are no longer full of themselves. They admit that God is God and they are not. The new life of Jesus restores them as the family of Seth and Noah.

The early Christians also live out Part 2 of the Bible. Luke informs us that they are *"unschooled, ordinary men"* – people who admit they are nobodies and who gamble everything on their belief that God is with them. They proclaim the message of Jesus' death and resurrection and, when thousands believe, they command them to be baptized and be added to God's Family.

Baptism was offensive to the Jews because it stated that being born of Abraham's bloodline did not make a person part of the Family of God. New Christians went underwater to express their faith that they had died and been buried with Jesus. They came up out of the water to express their faith that they had been raised to new life with Jesus in order to live the rest of their lives for him. It was as costly for the Jewish believers to be baptized as it was for Abraham to leave Ur of the Chaldees and set his face towards the Promised Land.

The early Christians also live out Part 3 of the Bible. They truly believe that God has saved them in order to dwell among them as his People. Jesus called his new community of followers the *Church*, using the same word which was used by the Greek Old Testament to refer to the *assembly* of Israelites which followed Moses in the desert. They therefore devote themselves to large-scale gatherings in the Temple courtyards and to small-scale gatherings in their homes – for preaching and worship and prayer and sharing bread and wine as their new Passover meal, a celebration of Jesus' death and resurrection. When Acts tells us that *"the Lord added to their number daily those who were being saved,"* it is not simply telling us that thousands of Jews believed in Jesus. It is telling us that they joined themselves to the new Christian community because they believed that it was the true fulfilment of the Jewish story.[4] They recognized that God was re-establishing his People at the heart of a city which had just crucified his Son.

The early Christians also live out Part 4 of the Bible. They start selling the land which was so precious to the Jews in order to use the money to lay hold of a greater Promised Land. They help the poorest Christians, ensuring that *"there was no needy person among them,"* and they tell the people of Jerusalem that Jesus has opened up new territory for his People. When Peter meets a lame man, he encourages him that healing is part of the message of new life. He heals him, telling him that healing is simply *"what I have."* Word spreads throughout Jerusalem that, in Jesus, a better Joshua has come. Very quickly, *"crowds gathered also from the towns around Jerusalem, bringing those who were ill and those tormented by impure spirits, and all of them were healed."* Living in Israel during the days of Joshua and conquering 8,000 square miles of land

---

4   Luke presents the Church as the continuation of the Jewish story in Acts 13:32–33; 24:14; 26:6–7; 28:20.

was exciting, but it was nothing compared to living in Jerusalem after Jesus' death and resurrection. Jesus leads God's People into a better Promised Land.

The early Christians also live out Parts 5 and 6 of the Bible. They listen to God's Word and they insist that they will always do things God's way. They take their guidance from the Old Testament Scriptures, convinced that Jesus is the true Messiah who has become the true heir of David, and they never stop *"proclaiming the good news that Jesus is the Messiah."* When the Jewish leaders act more like Eli and Saul than like Samuel and David, the Christians respond by using the psalms of David to pray for Christ's new Kingdom to be established. They tell those who oppose them that *"We must obey God rather than human beings!"* They describe themselves as followers of *"the Way"*.

The early Christians also live out Parts 7 and 8 of the Bible. They quote from the Old Testament prophets and act as warning sirens to the Jewish nation, saying that it has crucified God's Messiah. When its leaders refuse to listen, murdering God's prophets like the rebellious kings of Judah, Stephen follows the example of Jesus even as he dies. He cries out, *"Lord, do not hold this sin against them."* The biggest persecutor of the Church (a man who is appropriately named Saul) hears him. God uses Stephen's dying words to convict Saul and to set the stage for a very unlikely conversion. The God who broke out of the Jewish box by appearing to King Nebuchadnezzar of Babylon and by stirring the heart of King Cyrus of

Persia now appears to another great enemy of God's People. Saul is temporarily blinded by Jesus on the Road to Damascus but, as a result, he finally sees the big picture. He renames himself Paul and spearheads the global advance of the Gospel which was foretold by the Old Testament prophets.[5]

Luke expects us to see all this in the first nine chapters of Acts. He expects us to see that God has breathed new life into his great story. That's why these chapters echo Parts 1 to 8 of the Old Testament, and it is why they do not echo the message of Part 9. There is no disappointment in these chapters. The true and better Zerubbabel and Joshua has come, and he is building a new and better Temple. There is no lamenting while Jesus lays the foundations of the Church, because it is everything the prophets promised it would be and more.

The followers of Jesus discover that, through his death and resurrection and ascension, new life has now begun for the People of God.

---

5   King Saul was big-headed, so Saul renames himself Paul because it means *The-Little-Guy* in Latin. He takes the name from a Roman governor he meets on his travels (Acts 13:7–9). His new name helps him to connect with Gentiles.

PART 13
NO LIMITS

ACTS 10–28
37 AD TO 62 AD

It doesn't matter how powerful the electricity supply is. It only takes a single tripped switch to stop the current from flowing. In July 2012, a single isolator switch managed to cut off the power to 600 million people in India. Thirty-two gigawatts of electricity were ready to flow but a strip of insulation stopped the power from getting to where it was needed. That's what the Devil tries to do in Part 13 of the Bible. He tries to ring-fence and isolate the power of the new life which Jesus has provided for the world. God has to teach the early Christians to resist the Devil, because the Gospel message has no limits.

The Jews hated the Samaritans who had settled in the land after the destruction of the northern kingdom of Israel. Jesus challenged their racism, telling them that God's great story was as much for their semi-pagan neighbours as it was for themselves. In Acts

8, God thwarts the Devil's first attempt to insulate the Gospel by allowing Saul to persecute the early Christians and scatter them to the city of Samaria. They quickly discover that the message of new life in Jesus is just as powerful to save and heal Samaritans as it is to save and heal Jews. The disciple John had tried in Luke 9:54 to persuade Jesus to call down the fire of judgment on the Samaritans, so it is with deliberate irony that God chooses him to strip away the Devil's insulating tape of racism. God uses John to call down the fire of the Holy Spirit on Samaria. It's Jesus one, the Devil nil. The Devil cannot stop the power of the new life of Jesus from bursting through the first of his defensive barriers.

The Early Church is led by Peter, another of the twelve disciples and the former fishing partner of John. He is a strict Jew who scrupulously observes his nation's food laws and who looks like an easy ally in the Devil's plan to insulate the power of the Gospel from the world. When a Roman centurion sends a request for him to come and share the message of Jesus with a roomful of his Gentile friends, Peter would have refused outright had God not given him a vision in which he told him to eat pork and other meat forbidden to the Jews. Peter tells the centurion that *"You are well aware that it is against our law for a Jew to associate with or visit a Gentile. But God has shown me that I should not call anyone impure or unclean."*

Peter starts telling them about Jesus but, before he can finish, God suddenly fills the roomful of Romans with the Holy Spirit in the same way that he filled the

Jews and Samaritans. Some of the Jewish Christians are up in arms but Peter explains that he is simply following God's lead: *"If God gave them the same gift he gave us who believed in the Lord Jesus Christ, who was I to think that I could stand in God's way?"*[1] It's Jesus two, the Devil nil. The power of the new life of Jesus rushes on.

Luke loves writing about the church in Antioch because the power of the Gospel flowed out to him from that church even though he was a pagan doctor in the city. Saul chases the Christians as far north as Antioch and some of these fugitives break the biggest Jewish taboo. They preach the message of Jesus to this Gentile city without forcing their converts to embrace the trappings of Jewish culture along with the Gospel. Up until now, any non-Jew who wanted to convert to Israel's God needed to be circumcised and submit to the Jewish Law in all its detail, but the Jewish believers at Antioch make no such demands of their Greek converts. This sparks a debate which is only settled by a gathering in Jerusalem of all the Church's leaders in 49 AD.

The Devil tries to insulate the power of the Gospel by dressing it up in Jewish clothes, but the apostles decree that the Gentiles do not need to become Jews to become Christians. Since Jesus is the real Israel and he has fully obeyed the Jewish Law on our behalf, anyone who believes in him is deemed to have fulfilled the Jewish Law as well. They can follow Jesus in a manner which is appropriate to their own culture, as part of a glorious multi-ethnic expression of God's great

---

1   These two verses can be found in Acts 10:28; 11:17.

story of salvation. Although a group of false teachers continue to argue that all Christians must observe the Jewish Law, the Devil has failed to insulate the power of the Gospel. It's Jesus three, the Devil nil.

Paul becomes one of the leaders of the church at Antioch. This demonstrates that there are no limits to God's grace, since the church was planted as a direct result of Paul's earlier persecution of the Christians! The Lord chooses Paul to spearhead the campaign to plant churches like the one at Antioch in every city of the Greek-speaking world. The Devil tries to intimidate him through a powerful magician and to discourage him by making one of his teammates desert him. Paul is tempted to stop sharing the Gospel when his Jewish hearers get offended and his pagan hearers try to murder him. It looks for a moment as if the message of new life in Jesus will never gain a hearing with the stubborn Jews and clever pagans of the Greek heartland, but Paul refuses to let fear and failure trip an isolator switch in his heart.

Luke devotes over half of the book of Acts to the four missionary journeys of Paul because he wants to show us how Paul broke through the insulating barriers of the Devil to plant strong churches in every city throughout Cyprus, Turkey, Greece and Macedonia in the nine years from 48 to 57 AD. Luke outlines Paul's strategy in some detail because this is the point where he wants us to step into the story. He wants us to imitate Paul so that we can be as fruitful in spreading the Gospel in our generation as Paul was in his.

First, Luke tells us that Paul kept on preaching the message of new life in Jesus, even when he was threatened with death unless he toned down the exclusive claims of Jesus in the multi-faith Roman Empire. Paul tells his trainee Christian leaders in Acts 20:20–21 that *"You know that I have not hesitated to preach anything that would be helpful to you but have taught you publicly and from house to house. I have declared to both Jews and Greeks that they must turn to God in repentance and have faith in our Lord Jesus."* The Devil loves to persuade people that God's great story is just one of the great religious stories of the world. He loves to silence Christians through embarrassment and intimidation. But Paul assures us there is only one true God and only one true story of his salvation. If we want to see crowds turning to Jesus in our own generation, then we need to preach the same uncompromising message as Paul: Jesus is the only Saviour for the entire world.

Second, Luke tells us that Paul never shrank back from paying any price to declare the new life of Jesus to the world. Paul tells his trainee leaders in Acts 20:24 that *"I consider my life worth nothing to me; my only aim is to finish the race and complete the task the Lord Jesus has given me – the task of testifying to the good news of God's grace."* If you are too afraid or too distracted to tell other people about Jesus, then it shouldn't surprise you that God's mighty power never spreads from you to other people. Fear, busyness, self-centredness and a desire to play it safe are all very effective insulators against the Gospel. The book of Acts ends with Paul imprisoned in Rome because Luke wants us to realize that we now need to carry on his work in our own generation. It's Jesus four, the Devil nil at the end of the book of Acts, but there are still many more goals to be scored. If we pay the price to break through the Devil's insulation, then God's power will flow through us to reach a dying world with his new life.

Third, Luke tells us that Paul didn't just talk about the new life of Jesus. He also demonstrated that it is real. The book of Acts is full of miracles, and Paul tells us in Romans 15:18–19 that these were an essential factor in his success at spreading the Gospel: *"I will not venture to speak of anything except what Christ has accomplished through me in leading the Gentiles to obey God by what I have said and done – by the power of signs and wonders, through the power of the Spirit of God. So from Jerusalem all the way round to Illyricum, I have fully proclaimed the gospel of Christ."*

Paul tells us that demonstrating God's power through miracles is as much part of the Gospel as any spoken sermon. The new life of Jesus isn't just something for us to talk about, but something for us to enjoy. The Devil loves to restrict the flow of the Gospel by getting us to analyse and debate the resurrection of Jesus instead of demonstrating and proving it through works of power through the Holy Spirit. Paul was like Clint Eastwood at the end of a spaghetti western. He stood up to the Devil and to pagan idols in every city in the same way that Moses stood up to the idols of Egypt. He was quick on the draw to demonstrate that the power of Jesus is real and, as a result, people sat up and listened to the Gospel. His miracles of healing drew attention to his lifestyle and to his message. Luke tells us that our calling is to do the same.

It is Jesus four, the Devil nil, but the match continues. Will we follow in the footsteps of the early Christians and break through every barrier which the Devil builds to try to limit the spread of the Gospel? If we break through the barriers of racism, prejudice, cultural irrelevance, fear and discouragement, then the power of the Gospel will reach every nation of the world. If we preach the message of new life in Jesus in all its offensive glory, and if we demonstrate it in all its compelling power, then no obstacle will stand against us. We will break through every limitation which the Devil tries to use to insulate the world from the nation-changing power of the Gospel.

Part 13 of the Bible is exciting, but the way in which it ends is even more exciting. There is no proper ending to the book of Acts because Part 13 hasn't finished. Luke invites us to run onto the field and to play out the final chapters for ourselves. It's Jesus four, the Devil nil. Let's put on our boots and score some more goals of our own.

PART 14
YOU AND ME

ROMANS, 1&2 CORINTHIANS, GALATIANS, EPHESIANS, PHILIPPIANS, COLOSSIANS, 1&2 THESSALONIANS, 1&2 TIMOTHY, TITUS, PHILEMON, HEBREWS, JAMES, 1&2 PETER, 1,2&3 JOHN AND JUDE
48 AD TO 95 AD

Many people treat the Gospel in the same way they treat a software licence agreement. They don't study it in detail. They simply scroll down to the bottom and absent-mindedly click on "I agree". That's why twenty-one out of the twenty-seven books of the New Testament are letters written by the early Christian leaders to people like you and me. Part 14 of the Bible spells out for us why the Gospel is good news and what it means for us to experience the new life of Jesus in our daily lives.

The earliest of the twenty-one letters was probably written by James in about 48 AD. He was the half-brother of Jesus, the son of Mary and Joseph, and the leader of the team of elders which led the church in Jerusalem. He writes to the Jewish Christians scattered across the Roman Empire in order to give them a sampling of his sermons to the church in the Jewish capital. They strongly echo the book of Proverbs, as he reminds his congregation that following Jesus means living life God's way. *"Faith without deeds is useless,"* he warns us. *"As the body without the spirit is dead, so faith without deeds is dead."* The Gospel isn't an invitation to click lazily on "I agree". It is a command to die to our old way of living and to pledge ourselves to living God's way.

We do not know who wrote Hebrews, the only other New Testament letter which is addressed exclusively to Jewish Christians. All we know is that it was written by a Jewish church leader about three years before the Romans destroyed Jerusalem and its Temple in 70 AD. This would be a turning point in Jewish history – the Temple has never been rebuilt – but the writer of Hebrews prepares his readers to react to it very differently from the tragedy of 586 BC. There is no New Testament equivalent of the book of Lamentations because the arrival of Jesus the Messiah has marked a fundamental shift in God's great story. *"By calling this covenant 'new', he has made the first one obsolete; and what is obsolete and outdated will soon disappear,"* the writer tells the Jewish Christians. The details of the Law of Moses are now *"only a matter of food and drink and various ceremonial washings – external regulations applying until the time of the new order."* The Jewish Christians need not grieve when Jerusalem and its Temple are destroyed, as if they have no better hope. Those who follow Jesus have already *"come to Mount Zion, to the city of the living God, the heavenly Jerusalem."* Jesus has built the Church as a better Temple than the one built by Zerubbabel and as a better City than the one built by Nehemiah.[1]

Of the remaining nineteen letters, Peter wrote two, John wrote three and Jude (another half-brother of Jesus) wrote one. Jude's letter suggests that he worked as part of Peter's team, and John's letters are particularly important because they are dated the latest of the twenty-one letters. Writing as late as 95 AD, John assures a second and third generation of Christians that everything which they have read about Jesus in the gospels is true: *"That which was from the beginning, which we have heard, which we have seen with our eyes, which we have looked at and our hands have touched – this we proclaim concerning the Word of life. The life appeared; we have seen it and testify to it… We proclaim to you what we have seen and heard, so that you also may have fellowship with us."* Belief in the Gospel is not about ticking a box. It is about trusting in the one who has died and risen again in order to initiate us into his new life. John ends his first letter by telling us that *"I write these things to you who believe in the name of the Son of God so that you may know that you have eternal life."*[2]

The other thirteen letters were written by Paul: nine of them are to churches and four of them are to individual Christians. In and of itself, this showcases the power of the Gospel. The former persecutor of

1   See James 2:20, 26; Hebrews 8:13; 9:10; 12:22.
2   1 John 1:1–3; 5:13.

the Church became the writer of half of the books in the New Testament and the greatest shaper of our understanding of the new life which we have in Jesus.

Paul is still passionate about the Jewish race and he insists that the Gospel is given *"first to the Jew, then to the Gentile."*[3] He tells us that, before God's great story ends, the Jews will become jealous that so many Gentiles are enjoying new life through Israel's God. Large numbers of Jews will turn to Jesus as their Messiah and be saved. Nevertheless, the big message of Galatians is that Gentile believers must not be saddled with the Jewish Law, and one of the big messages of Ephesians is that those who were *"excluded from citizenship in Israel and foreigners to the covenants of the promise, without hope and without God in the world... who once were far away have been brought near by the blood of Christ. For he himself is our peace, who has made the two groups one... For through him we both have access to the Father by one Spirit."* Those who skim over the detail of the Gospel in order to click on "I agree" miss out on the depth of what new life in Jesus really means.

Paul spends large sections of his letters ensuring that we understand who we are now that we have received the new life of Jesus. He tells us that God chose us before the beginning of time and that our faith has united us with Jesus. We died with Jesus, we were buried with Jesus, we were raised with Jesus and we have ascended to heaven to sit with Jesus at God's right hand. Paul tells us that God wants to fill

3   These quotations from Paul's letters can be found in Romans 1:16; 9:1–9; 11:11–32; Ephesians 2:11–22.

us completely with his Holy Spirit so that the same power which raised the corpse of Jesus from the dead will also bring life to our mortal bodies. Paul's letters have inspired tens of thousands of worship songs over the years. The more we read the small print of the Gospel, the more grateful to God we become and the more we want to praise him.

Paul also spends large sections of his letters ensuring that we understand what it means to live out the new life we have received in Jesus. Since we have been raised with Jesus, everything about the way we live our lives now needs to change. We need to turn from every idol and we need to offer our bodies as living sacrifices to Jesus. We need to let the Holy Spirit work the character of Jesus into our hearts, making us better parents and children and workers and employers and leaders and citizens and neighbours. We need to let the Holy Spirit give us the power of Jesus through spiritual gifts which help us to reach and help a lost and dying world. Paul assures us that the same gifts which he exercises in the book of Acts are still available for you and for me. They will be available right up until the moment when God brings his great human story to an end.[4]

Paul also spends large sections of his letters showing us how to steward the message of new life in Jesus up until that day. He shows us how to resist the Devil's tricks, how to pray, how to share the Gospel with others, how to make disciples and how to build healthy churches which reproduce themselves all

---

4   Paul says these gifts will last until Jesus returns and we see him *"face to face"* (1 Corinthians 1:7; 13:9–12).

across the world. *"The gospel is bearing fruit and growing throughout the whole world,"* he reminds us. *"Be wise in the way you act towards outsiders; make the most of every opportunity."*[5]

These twenty-one letters are so jam-packed with the small print of the Gospel that they should captivate our attention for a lifetime. The more we read, the more we understand. The more we understand, the more we want to worship. The more we worship, the more we find ourselves equipped to carry on the work which Paul and the other writers of the New Testament began. So don't miss the big picture of Part 14 of the Bible. God gives us twenty-one personal letters instead of twenty-one cold lectures because the Gospel is not an invitation to scroll through a list of words and click on "I agree". It is an invitation to dive into the new life of Jesus and apply it to every area of our lives.

God's great story isn't over. It is still being played out in your life and in mine. That's why Part 14 of the Bible consists of twenty-one letters. They were written for you and me.

---

5   Colossians 1:6; 4:5.

PART 15
END OF STORY

REVELATION
100 AD TO THE SECOND COMING OF JESUS

Old age is never easy, but for John it was a living nightmare. He lived to be about a hundred years of age and his final years were not pleasant ones. Things became so difficult for the Church that he started wondering whether it was the end of the story for God's People.

By 95 AD, all of the original twelve disciples were dead, except for John. They had been beheaded or crucified or worse. Despite his extreme old age, John had been banished to the Greek island of Patmos, where he heard snippets of news that thousands of ordinary Christians were being martyred by the Romans. In addition to this persecution on the outside, the Church had been infected with false teaching, immorality and corruption on the inside. We can tell that John must have felt a bit like we do when we look around us today and see a Church so weak that it makes us doubt the message of Acts and the New Testament letters. We can tell that he must have been tempted to succumb to disappointment and despair, because God gave him some amazing encouragement. He gave him a vision of Jesus which was so powerful that it became the final book of the New Testament. Revelation is Part 15 of the Bible, the final part of God's great story.

In Revelation 1, John describes what he saw of Jesus. God draws back the curtain to reveal what is really going on in heaven behind the troubled scenes of history. John knew Jesus as he is revealed in the four gospels better than anyone – he wrote one of the gospels! He knew Jesus as a humble carpenter, as a sinless man, as God's suffering sacrifice and as the risen Lord. But this wasn't enough to keep him trusting in the Gospel throughout the highs and lows of history. He was tempted to think that it was the end of the story for God's People – until he saw a vision of Jesus as he is right now in heaven. The ascended King of kings who reigns on heaven's Throne in undisputed glory is far too powerful to fail. John leaned on Jesus' chest at the Last Supper, but he confesses that this had not prepared him for a glimpse of Jesus in all his glory: *"His face was like the sun shining in all its brilliance. When I saw him, I fell at his feet as though dead."*[6] Part 15 of the Bible prepares us to walk through the highs and lows of AD history, safe in the knowledge that Jesus is always in control – end of story.

In Revelation 2 and 3, Jesus dictates seven letters to seven churches in the Roman province of

---

6   The verses quoted in this chapter can be found in Revelation 1:16–17; 5:9; 7:9–10; 21:3–5; 22:20.

Asia. These were real churches, but Jesus uses their condition to prepare us for the state of the Church throughout history. There will be times when the Church loses her first love and appears lukewarm and asleep, but we must not fool ourselves that this means it is "game over" for the Gospel. Jesus fills these seven letters with allusions to the Old Testament history of Israel because he wants to reassure us that he is just as sovereign over the events of AD history as he was over the events of BC history. Jesus ends each letter with a promise about what he will do for us if we stay faithful and persevere. We will live with him forever in paradise and eat from the tree of life which Adam lost. We will eat better manna than Moses and enjoy a better Kingdom than David. We will be part of a better Temple than was built by Solomon and a better city than was built by Nehemiah. The unfaithfulness of Christians cannot ruin God's big picture.

In Revelation 4–5, John sees a vision of what is happening in heaven. He sees that Jesus is the slaughtered Lamb of God and that he alone has power to open up the book of history. He alone will shape the final chapter in the human story. The Devil may attack the Church and attempt to insulate the power of the Gospel, but he cannot stop the song of praise to Jesus which resounds through heaven: *"with your blood you purchased for God persons from every tribe and language and people and nation."*

In Revelation 6–7, John watches Jesus break each of the Seven Seals which represent his sovereign power to shape the book of history. Despite the

Devil's best attempts to destroy the human race, God always has the last word in the story. He can even turn around for good war and famine and disease and persecution. Jesus will ensure that the bitter pain of world history has a sweet and happy ending. John looks up and sees that *"there before me was a great multitude that no one could count, from every nation, tribe, people and language, standing before the throne and before the Lamb... And they cried out in a loud voice: 'Salvation belongs to our God, who sits on the throne, and to the Lamb.'"* Part 15 of the Bible warns us upfront that history will be hard at times as we wait for Jesus to return, but it also promises us that Jesus rules from the throne room of heaven.

In Revelation 8–20, John sees the events of AD history unfold over and over again, represented by the blowing of Seven Trumpets and the pouring out of Seven Bowls. He describes them in apocalyptic language, an ancient genre which Daniel 12:10 says was deliberately obscure so that *"None of the wicked will understand, but those who are wise will understand."* God wants us to understand that the Church will look very weak for long periods of history. At times, it will even look as though the Church is dead and the Devil has won. But if God's master plan to save the world involved his own Son suffering and dying, we should not grow discouraged as if this could ever truly be the end of the story. In Revelation 20, God defeats the Devil and throws him into hell for ever. Those who are thrown into hell because they sided with him and rejected the promise of new life in Jesus have no excuse. God has given us so much time to repent that none of us can complain that God is being unfair when the story finally ends.

Revelation 21–22 is the glorious grand finale of the Bible. Having dealt decisively with evil on the Day of Judgment, God can now give us a glimpse of the paradise which awaits those who follow him. He promises that he will recreate the world as it was always intended to be before Adam and Eve sinned. Heaven will come down to earth and he will fuse the two together into one glorious place where God will dwell with his People for ever. The Lord shouts in triumph from his Throne at the end of Revelation: *"Look! God's dwelling-place is now among the people, and he will dwell with them. They will be his people, and God himself will be with them and be their God. 'He will wipe every tear from their eyes. There will be no more death' or mourning or crying or pain, for the old order of things has passed away… 'I am making everything new!'"*

That's the end of the story. That's where world history is heading. That's the grand finale to a story which has taken us through 66 books, 1,189 chapters and 31,102 verses. We discover that the whole of BC and AD history has simply formed the prelude to the eternal life which we will enjoy with Jesus throughout all eternity. God loves us so much that he likens our eternal relationship with Jesus to that of a beaming bride and groom when they are finally joined together on their wedding day. God is so committed to saving the nations that he reveals to John that the New Jerusalem is a city so large, it measures 2.75 billion cubic miles in size.

There will be setbacks. There will be times when God's great story appears to have come to an end. But don't let that make you miss the big picture. God is on the Throne and he is sovereignly shaping the events of world history to fulfil his master plan to save the world. *"I am coming soon,"* Jesus tells us as the Bible draws to an end. Let's respond with John: *"Amen. Come, Lord Jesus."*

God is on the Throne. His great plan to save the world will succeed completely – end of story.

CONCLUSION: BURN AFTER READING

On an autumn day in 1536, a man named William Tyndale was burned at the stake in a castle courtyard a few miles away from the Belgian city of Brussels. His crime? He was the first man to translate the Bible from Hebrew and Greek into ordinary English so that his entire nation could discover God's great story for themselves. You have just finished reading a 100-page overview of the book for which William Tyndale was willing to die. He burned so that you might be able to read.

This little book is meant to help you to grasp the big picture of God's great story, but it isn't meant to be a substitute for reading the Bible itself. William Tyndale was executed because the ruling classes were enraged that he was smuggling Bibles into England, hiding them inside the sacks of corn which were imported from the harvest fields of Belgium. The sixteenth-century English were not content to hear the big picture of the Bible preached in their churches every Sunday. They were willing to risk everything to lay their own hands on a Bible and to read it every day. Six hundred of them would be executed in the two decades which followed the burning of William Tyndale.

You are about to finish this little book. The question is: *What will you do as a result?* Will you slip back into a culture which is busy with many things which do not really matter, or will you burn with a passion to dive into the Bible and discover God's great story in much more detail?

To help you, I have written a series of devotional commentaries on the Bible in a similar style to *The Bible in 100 Pages*. If you have enjoyed this little book, then you will find these commentaries very helpful, taking you through each of the sixty-six books of the Bible in turn. They will explain to you what each book says, challenge you to face up to what that means, and help you to apply that challenge to your life. You can find all of the books in the *Straight to the Heart* series of commentaries at any good book retailer, or by visiting **www.philmoorebooks.com**

This particular book was based on a series of sermons which I preached at Everyday Church, the church I lead in London, England. All of our preaching is rooted in the Bible for which William Tyndale gave his life to translate it into our language. We make our sermons available online free of charge, both as videos and as audio files, in order to help people to dive deeper into God's great story. If you think that this might help you, you can find all of our latest sermons at **www.everyday.org.uk/sermons**

I also use Twitter to help people follow Jesus every day. You can find these tweets by searching for **@philmoorelondon**

William Tyndale was burned at the stake and died because of his passion for the Bible, but God wants you to be set on fire with a passion to live for the Bible and to proclaim its message to a lost and dying world. In the eighteenth century, John Wesley led one of the greatest Christian revivals in the history of the English-speaking world. Millions of people around the world became followers of Jesus because of his fearless preaching of the message of the Bible. When people asked him how he managed to draw such crowds, he told them: *"I set myself on fire and people came to watch me burn."* Because he set himself on fire with passion to study the Bible and to preach its message, he was able to write in a letter to one of his friends: *"The Word of the Lord runs and is glorified, and his work goes on and prospers. Great multitudes are everywhere awakened and cry out, 'What must we do to be saved?'"*

William Tyndale is dead. John Wesley is dead. But you and I live on. What are you going to do with the message you have discovered in the pages of the Bible? Will you let the big picture of God's great story set you on fire? Will you see this little book as a mere springboard which helps you dive far deeper into the detail of the Bible?

If you want God to walk with you as he walked with Noah, then read the Bible. If you want God to speak to you as he spoke to Abraham, then read the Bible. If you want God to guide you as he guided Moses, then read the Bible. If you want God to deliver you as he delivered David, then read the Bible. If you want God to make you as fruitful as he made Paul and the other early Christian leaders, then read the Bible. God is God and we are not, so in the Bible he has provided us with all the help we need to play the privileged role which he has given us in his story.

That's the big picture. That's the message of the Bible. What you do with that message now is up to you.

STRAIGHT TO THE HEART SERIES

TITLES AVAILABLE: OLD TESTAMENT

STRAIGHT TO THE HEART OF
Genesis
60 BITE-SIZED INSIGHTS
Phil Moore

ISBN 978 0 85721 001 2

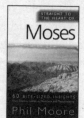

STRAIGHT TO THE HEART OF
Moses
60 BITE-SIZED INSIGHTS
Phil Moore

ISBN 978 0 85721 056 2

STRAIGHT TO THE HEART OF
1&2 Samuel
60 BITE-SIZED INSIGHTS
Phil Moore

ISBN 978 0 85721 252 8

STRAIGHT TO THE HEART OF
Psalms
60 BITE-SIZED INSIGHTS
Phil Moore

ISBN 978 0 85721 428 7

STRAIGHT TO THE HEART OF
Solomon
60 BITE-SIZED INSIGHTS
Phil Moore

ISBN 978 0 85721 426 3

AND IN THE
SAME SERIES AS
**THE BIBLE IN
100 PAGES**

GAGGING JESUS
THINGS JESUS SAID WE WISH HE HADN'T
PHIL MOORE

ISBN 978 0 85721 453 9

TITLES AVAILABLE: NEW TESTAMENT

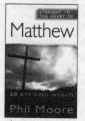

STRAIGHT TO THE HEART OF
Matthew
60 BITE-SIZED INSIGHTS
Phil Moore

ISBN 978 1 85424 988 3

STRAIGHT TO THE HEART OF
John
60 BITE-SIZED INSIGHTS
Phil Moore

ISBN 978 0 85721 253 5

STRAIGHT TO THE HEART OF
Acts
60 BITE-SIZED INSIGHTS
Phil Moore

ISBN 978 1 85424 989 0

STRAIGHT TO THE HEART OF
Romans
60 BITE-SIZED INSIGHTS
Phil Moore

ISBN 978 0 85721 057 9

STRAIGHT TO THE HEART OF
1&2 Corinthians
60 BITE-SIZED INSIGHTS
Phil Moore

ISBN 978 0 85721 002 9

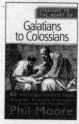

STRAIGHT TO THE HEART OF
Galatians to Colossians
60 BITE-SIZED INSIGHTS FROM GALATIANS, EPHESIANS, PHILIPPIANS, COLOSSIANS AND PHILEMON
Phil Moore

ISBN 978 0 85721 546 8

STRAIGHT TO THE HEART OF
1 Thessalonians to Titus
60 BITE-SIZED INSIGHTS FROM 1&2 THESSALONIANS, 1&2 TIMOTHY
Phil Moore

ISBN 978 0 85721 548 2

STRAIGHT TO THE HEART OF
Revelation
60 BITE-SIZED INSIGHTS
Phil Moore

ISBN 978 1 85424 990 6